Anne Brontë
Educating Parents

Mary Summers

Highgate of Beverley

Highgate Publications (Beverley) Limited
2003

Acknowledgements

I should like to express my gratitude for the encouragement I received from Dr. Mary Waldron, Dr. Lois Chaber and Dr. Carol Banks of the Women's Study Group, University of London, and also from Mrs. Joan Bellamy, Mr. Bob Duckett and Dr. Robert Barnard of the Brontë Society.

I am also indebted to my husband and my mother for supporting me during the two years of writing this book and my son, Mark, for his constant and cheerful agreement to proof-read.

My thanks go too to Ann Dinsdale of The Brontë Society Library for allowing me access to some of the child drawings by Anne Brontë, and to St. Mary's Scarborough P.C.C. for allowing a copy of a print showing Anne Brontë's burial place to be used in this book.

The Cover photograph is reproduced by kind permission of the Brontë Parsonage Museum.

British Library Cataloguing in Publication Data.
A catalogue record for this book is available from the British Library.

© 2003 Mary Summers

Mary Summers asserts the moral right to be identified as the author of this work.

ISBN 1 902645 36 7

Published by

Highgate of Beverley

Highgate Publications (Beverley) Limited
4 Newbegin, Beverley, HU17 8EG. Telephone (01482) 886017

Printed by Highgate Print Limited
4 Newbegin, Beverley, HU17 8EG. Telephone (01482) 886017

Contents

Illustrations

Texts and Abbreviations

AG *Agnes Grey*, ed. Temple Scott (John Grant, 1911).

TWH *The Tenant of Wildfell Hall*, ed. G. D. Hargreaves, intro.
Winifred Gérin, (Penguin Books, 1979).

The Edward Chitham edition of *The Poems of Anne Brontë* has been
used throughout.

Introduction

'Then I may cherish at my breast
An infant's form beloved and fair,
May smile and soothe it into rest
With all a mother's fondest care'
(Anne Brontë: *'Dreams'*.)

From Anne Brontë's poetry, novels and schoolgirl drawings of babies
in 1837, and from her watercolour, in 1843, of a delightful, fair-haired
little girl (who could well have resembled her as a child), it is not
difficult to ascertain that what she most longed for in life was a loving
relationship as a wife and mother of children, for whose upbringing
she, as a parent, would have been responsible. For many reasons this
was not to be, one of which might well concern William Weightman's
premature death, and another, the simple fact of there being more
women than men around at the time she lived, so making the odds
very great against a young lady however charming, though without a
dowry, of finding a husband. Anne's only alternative, if she wished to
retain the independence of spirit she so valued, was to become an
educator of other people's children and thereby offer them the many
gifts she possessed.

Anne did not put forward her thoughts on the important role of a
wife and mother in rearing children according to Christian principles
until she had reached a decisive point in her life. Her brother,
Branwell, was in the midst of his three-year-long illness, self-induced
by disappointment, drink and drugs, when she began her novels. His
suffering and the waste of his talents helped her overcome her natural
reserve and increased her resolve to publicize her ideas in her two
novels, *Agnes Grey* and *The Tenant of Wildfell Hall*. Her views on the
need for women to be better educated were based on common-
sensical, practical ideas, which she had gleaned from her background,
her reading and her work experience as a governess. From what she
witnessed with her two sets of employers, the Inghams and the
Robinsons, she had become fully aware of the dangers of entering too
lightly into matrimony and motherhood, where the laws of the land
prevented women from any escape. Consequently, she decided to
translate her heart-felt thoughts and experience into the medium of

art in order to warn her readers of the dangers of succumbing to such snares and temptations without serious reflection.

Her nature was such as to conceal her thoughts, and, as Charlotte put it in her Biographical Notice of Ellis and Acton Bell, in 1850, the three sisters were 'averse to personal publicity'. However, she overrode the delicacy of her nature by her sheer determination to benefit others. One can well imagine her great disappointment at the reception of her second novel, *The Tenant of Wildfall Hall,* which contemporary critics, including her sister Charlotte, failed to appreciate, when she had sacrificed her privacy to promote her sensible, God-fearing advice to help others attain the loving relationship which had been denied her.

Her first novel, *Agnes Grey,* is indeed a 'conduct book' targeting anyone involved in the educating or the upbringing of children. This would include unmarried spinsters, like herself who had ended up, through lack of choice, as governesses; ladies contemplating marriage and future motherhood; and those already married and who were already parents or about to become so. Anne opposed the conditioning process of her age which demanded that parents rear their children to comply unquestioningly with the exigencies of their times, and certainly not to use their reasoning powers to make informed judgments in life. Her novels seek to promote a different kind of education from that practised by Victorian society, more akin to the ideas of eighteenth-century writers such as Hannah More, Mary Brunton, Jane Austen and even Mary Wollstonecraft. *Agnes Grey* is written by someone who has practised what she is preaching, in fact by a real-life educator. Anne's opinions are voiced by her fictional governess, Agnes, who is seen to share her aim to transform her pupils through education so that subsequently they might play a part in the transformation of their own children's ideas, effecting consequently, through the continuity of such a cycle of instruction, a gradual, yet quiet revolutionary change in the attitude of current and future generations towards their young.

In *The Tenant of Wildfell Hall,* Anne's approach is more overtly Evangelical and her ideas on Universal Salvation are propagated as freely as is her advice to the married and unmarried on how to resolve the problems of oppression of women in their male dominated society.

The main thrust of Anne's argument is directed at those holding parental responsibility, warning them of the dangers in store for them if they do not adhere to the immensely practical guide-lines and principles she sets out so clearly and so amusingly in the form of illustrations taken from everyday life. Her instructions are based on her own upbringing and her extensive reading and also, according to Charlotte come 'from the impulse of nature, the dictates of intuition, and from such stores of observation', as her experience of working for gentry had allowed her to amass. As such they suggest, rather than tell the reader, of this need to change the way in which men and women are educated. She so wanted to bring forth a new race of reasoning, self-controlled and highly principled beings. Anne's dream can be interpreted as her wish that eventually, through the educational transformation she so desires, a new ideal society will emerge, where men and women, the latter no longer viewed just as domestic possessions but rather as beings capable of independent thought, would live together in companionship and intellectual equality, rearing their families in peace and harmony. As Hannah More put it, a woman in marriage should be to her husband 'a friend, a companion, and a wife'.

Anne Brontë, drawn by her sister, Charlotte.

By permission of the Brontë Society Parsonage Museum.

Chapter 1:

Parents are patterns

'All the Brontës deal with love in their work;
Anne alone is concerned with parenthood.'
(E. Chitham: *A Life of Anne Brontë*)

Anne Brontë was unmarried, childless, the youngest in the family, and without any experience of bringing up siblings. On the basis of such facts, one might well be forgiven for questioning the relevance of her views on rearing a child, as her credentials for supplying informative guide-lines on this subject do indeed look decidedly shaky. However, a closer look at her background; at her experience as pupil, governess and would-be teacher in her own school; at her observational powers and strong imagination, and also at her ideas, as revealed in her poetry and her two novels, *Agnes Grey* and *The Tenant of Wildfell Hall*, and at how these ideas were influenced by those of various writers, proves helpful in reversing this impression and in revealing why Anne's brave decision to expound her theories in her writings, provides useful advice even for the parent of the twenty-first century.

Yet, how could someone who has often been portrayed as timid be courageous enough to convey, through her writings, a sharp reprimand to society on such sensitive issues as the laws enforced on women, and women's education or what Brontë considered their lack of it? Many biographers have challenged this idea of her being shy, including Winifred Gerin, who calls her 'a resolute-minded and highly courageous young woman',[1] even though her sister, Charlotte insists on her being thought of as timid and viewed her as 'resigned' and 'gentle'.[2] An example of the strength of Anne's will-power emerges when she is offered a free place as pupil at Roe Head, gained as a result of Charlotte's services as a teacher at the school. Her sister, Emily, Charlotte's first choice to take up the place, proves unable to bear being separated from her home and family, and so returns to the Parsonage. The offer then passes to her youngest sister. In complete opposition to her father's wish to keep her at home for a further year, (as expressed in his letter of June 1835 to Mrs. Franks), Anne Brontë, through her sheer determination to take advantage of the education on offer, manages to persuade him to allow her to accompany Charlotte back to Roe Head in October 1835. This same independence of thought is voiced in her first novel, *Agnes Grey,* through her fictional governess, Agnes, whose reasoning power overcomes parental opposition to become a governess. Another example, this one taken from real life, is when Anne resigns in June 1845 from her post as governess with her second employers, the Robinsons. She takes this decision to leave Thorp Green, (where, as she says in her diary paper of 31 July, 1845: 'during my stay I have had some very unpleasant and undreamt of experience of human nature') entirely independently of her sisters' advice, as is evident from her having to announce it to them on her arrival home in late June. Also, in one of her Gondal poems, written in 1845, ten years after her departure for Roe Head School, called Parting Address from Z.Z. to A.E., Anne's will-power and steely strength of character can again be glimpsed, successfully concealed by her poetic persona: 'Fear not for me – I've steeled my mind to combat all'. And in the last stanza she adds: 'I will not break my vow'. As additional proof of her strength of character, her portrait of Agnes Grey reveals an Agnes filled with an inner force, attributable, for the most part, to her reliance on God and on truth. If Anne's utterances in her writings, especially in *Agnes Grey,* are accepted as being even semi-autobiographical, it becomes apparent that she is describing how writing is both 'a relief' and 'a secret source of consolation' to her, and that she views her poems as a recollection and preservation of 'past sufferings and experience, like pillars of witness set up in travelling through the vale of life to mark particular occurrences.' Anne, shielded by Agnes, voices her own opinions, and powerful feelings which, otherwise, her love of concealment of her emotions would not have allowed her to make public, as in her poem entitled *A Fragment* of 1 January, 1840, where she says: 'They could not read my secret thoughts, nor see my throbbing heart.'

She translates into art her anxieties at what she perceives to be happening around her in her own family and in Victorian society, in an attempt to find the answer to her worries, which she sets in print as 'pillars of witness' to the events in question. She uses both poetry and prose to interpret, photograph and hence commit to memory her thoughts and feelings about people and events, a form of secret diary of her own life, which is veiled to others, to whom it appears as fiction. In fact, Anne's own diary does remain secret, for unfortunately only a few extracts of it remain in the form of diary papers. She mentions two more secret diaries, both fictional, one which is kept by Agnes Grey and one which is that of Helen Huntingdon in *The Tenant of Wildfell Hall.* Helen's attitude towards keeping her diary secret, by locking it away to avoid public gaze, especially that of her husband, is revelatory of Anne's own attitude towards hers.

Her writing is a vehicle for truth as she understands it, for she cannot be silent on certain issues. Indeed, the therapeutic, soothing qualities of her poetic outpourings help her to express both her anxieties, frustrations and dreams, and even to attempt to work out solutions. As is especially evident in some of her personal poems, Anne constantly indulges in self-examination throughout her writings, as did Mary Wollstonecraft in her early writings. Both writers were searching for self-knowledge and answers to their questions, following closely on the Lockean assumption that all knowledge of every kind is derived from an interrogation of experience and memory. An example of such self-analysis can be glimpsed in her poem, *To Cowper,* written on the 10 November 1842, after her father's curate, William Weightman, had died in September and just after her aunt's funeral on 3 November. She had just discovered that Cowper, one of her favourite poets, had, like her brother Branwell, spent many sad moments during his life doubting whether he was indeed saved. Anne says of him:

> 'I did not know the nights of gloom,
> The days of misery.
> The long long years of dark despair
> That crushed and tortured thee'.

She counters Cowper's worries in this poem by praying that he is with God, saying: 'It must be so if God is love.' Indeed, she argues out the case for his salvation, carefully refuting his anxieties, but then ends her poem by expressing doubts as to whether her own heart was 'of Heavenly grace bereft'. She says that if 'such a soul' as his was lost, how indeed would she appear to God?' Such self-questioning was to continue until this whole issue of personal salvation could be resolved in her mind,

By the time she began writing *The Tenant* in 1847, Anne felt convinced enough of her arguments to state her opposition, through her use of authentic imagery and situations, to the consequences of a lack of values and parental discipline in boys' and girls' education. Had she not, by then, already experienced such consequences in the life of her own brother, Branwell? As Charlotte said of her in the Biographical Notice of Ellis and Acton Bell, on 19 September, 1850, which she wrote over two years after her sister's death: 'She had, in the course of her life been called on to contemplate, near at hand, and for a long time, the terrible effects of talents misused and faculties abused'. One can easily understand Anne Brontë's deep disappointment, as revealed in her so-called Preface to the Second edition of her second novel in 1848, at her aim being so sadly misunderstood by contemporary, literary critics, who accused her of cruelty and coarseness of subject matter – features so alien to her nature – when indeed what she really wanted to do was, as Charlotte noted, 'to reproduce every detail (of course with fictitious characters, incidents, and situations) as a warning to others'.[3] Most probably, while writing *The Tenant*, she had already had to endure pressure from Charlotte to change her subject and so it was a double blow to her to know that contemporary critics also found it difficult to comprehend the purpose of her novel.

In short, Anne was offering her readers – parents, grandparents and teachers of children alike – the whole process, as she saw it, by which to bring up children and rear them in true Christian fashion, by imparting to them a strong code of biblical values and thereby a pattern by which to live. Her advice did not stop short at children but was also aimed at the parents themselves, for she sought to instruct them on how best to relate to each other in marriage and to their children, by offering them sound, moral guide-lines along the lines of a conduct book. Indeed, both her novels reveal how deeply she feels these marital and parental relationships are interlinked and how, in essence, relationship provides the clue to a good upbringing and thereby, eventually, to a lessening of the ills of society caused by bad parenting.

However, the art of parenting is hardly a subject that has ever tended to figure over-much on the school curriculum. Even by the mid-twentieth century, parents were still relying either on their own parents for tips or hunting through Child Psychology books, such as Winnicot, Bowlby or even Dr. Spock, for any advice they could find on how to bring up their infants. Such books usually concentrated more on the child's mental and physical progress, particularly the reaching of rigid stages of development as revealed by Piaget, than on the more spiritual side of building up a relationship between parent and child within the family. Yet, strangely enough, when we look back through the eyes of Anne Brontë at the main issues of parenting as she saw them in the nineteenth century, it becomes evident that where she places her emphasis is on this very factor of relationship. She stresses courageously the responsibility of the parent before God to educate 'a soul for heaven' airing her views through her protagonists, Agnes Grey and Helen Huntingdon. It is Helen who defines the relationship that, in Brontë's opinion, ought to exist between a parent and child: 'my comfort and my joy, and me to be his shield, instructor, friend – to guide him along the perilous path of youth, and train him to be God's servant while on earth, a blessed and honoured saint in heaven.' (TWH, p.252).

In her writings, Anne implies her concern for the lack of respect or love between parents, which influences not only their own relationships but also those they have with their children. Undoubtedly, her thoughts are based in part on her observation of the marriages within her sphere including those of her father's parishioners, her aunts and uncles, and of her own two sets of employers, the Inghams and the Robinsons, whose uninterested approach to forming a relationship with each other or with their children very much saddened her. She notes the reasons why these relationships had failed as being the lack of informative guide-lines given to the women involved and the way in which, in arranging a marriage for their children, her employers' personal priority fell on monetary gain and eligibility of status rather than on mutual love or respect. In *Agnes Grey,* we see an example of this, in Agnes's pupil, Rosalie Murray, who is totally ignorant of the world and conditioned by her mother to put her faith in external attributes, such as her beauty rather than in the improvement of her mind. Under her mother's mercenary influence, she agrees to be allied with her parents' choice of a wealthy suitor, an utterly debauched rascal, complete, however, with title and handsome estate. Rosalie, totally unprepared by her mother for making any sound decision on marriage, rejects Agnes's advice to reflect well before making her choice for, in her ignorance, she is convinced that the way her mother advocates has to be the right one and, once wed, she will be able to reform Sir Thomas Ashby and live happily with him ever after. In vain does Agnes try to work against the preconceived ideas of the age, which have been passed on from mother to daughter such as: 'reformed rakes make the best husbands, everybody knows' (TWH, p.184) and the marriage takes place with, as Agnes has indicated, disastrous consequences.

Although by the nineteenth century marriages were not all arranged, there still existed the strongly held feeling in Victorian society that a marriage partner ought to conform with the parents' choice and that choice should always be a 'sensible' one, increasing, if possible, one's social position or wealth. Anne hits out here at these 'marriages of convenience', contracted for financial or social reasons instead of love, and at the lack of relationship and decidedly poor communication which existed between mother and child, with daughters receiving no guidance worth speaking of on how to choose their future life partner, other than to follow blindly riches and status. Evidently, strength of character, goodness and gentleness in a man were not the qualities advocated by such parents. No matter how depraved the wealthy suitor might be, his high position in society could always render him eligible! Indeed, mothers seemed more than content to accept unflinchingly the sacrifice of uninformed daughters to any rich (therefore suitable) 'rakes' as an exchange of innocence for future provision. This idea of inexperience being valued in a wife, who could not be too ignorant, had been used as a literary theme for at least the last two centuries. Indeed, this very theme of ignorance and the unpreparedness of girls to meet the challenges of life is also challenged by Anne in her second novel, where her fictional heroine, Helen, is also seen to ignore her aunt's very good advice not to marry Arthur Huntingdon, failing to realise that any attempt to reform him will fall on deaf ears. In addition, her friend, Milicent Hargrave, inveigled by the machinations of her mother rather than being trained to think for herself, is also seen to allow herself to be forced into a marriage for money with a man she does not love. Elizabeth Gaskell describes similar ideas on marriage in her novel, *Wives and Daughters,* where the ostentatious Hyacinth Kirkpatrick only agrees to marry Dr. Gibson to better her financial position and certainly not out of love, and is only prised out of her self-interest by the thought that she might be able to get rid of her only daughter, Cynthia, to a wealthy and therefore, in her eyes, totally acceptable suitor. The issue as to whether Cynthia has any affection for the various men who present themselves as her suitors fails to interest or concern her at all. Indeed, such ideas seem totally incomprehensible to her. Fortunately, by the time this second marriage of Hyacinth with Dr. Gibson takes place, his daughter by his first marriage, Molly, has already reached an age of some discretion, having been soundly educated beforehand along Christian lines of behaviour both by her father and her late mother's friends, the Miss Brownings, so Molly manages to resist her step-mother's pernicious influence.

On this aspect of the need for women to have enough knowledge to make an informed choice it was most probably the young Mary Wollstonecraft and Hannah More who influenced Anne the most, for there are very decided echoes in her two novels of More's insistent views 'that a young woman should be well-informed' but should not push her knowledge on others, nor use her cleverness 'to attempt to exercise power.' More says she must be able to join in the conversation when required, but to leave the leadership to the man.[4] Such ideas are certainly followed, later on, by Charlotte M. Yonge in her 1865 novel, *The Clever Woman of the Family*, where the heroine, Rachel Curtis, blames such behaviour on the fact that she had neither 'father or brother to keep me in order.'[5] Hence, her relationships fail constantly as she exhibits her cleverness and her cynical attitude to faith, whereas Ermine Williams, the really 'clever woman' of the novel, is truly devout and knows when to speak and when to hold her tongue.

Anne emphasises a need to educate children from within the family, from the earliest age on, by imparting to them sound values to aid in the formation of their characters. Indeed, she suggests in *Agnes Grey* that infants readily absorb what they see around them and take on the characteristics of their parents or of those who are in loco parentis, for parents are indeed patterns. They learn how to relate to others from within their family situation, from the ways in which their parents, brothers and sisters act or behave towards each other and towards them. If no genuine adherence to a value system can be perceived on the part of the parents, neither can one be readily transmitted to the children. Anne remarks on how parents' outer semblance of concern with virtue can be easily discerned as insincere by their children, and passed on as such. In Anne's estimation, fathers and mothers who deny time and affection to train their young in the best way to proceed in life cause their children and themselves unnecessary suffering. Throughout her writings, the reader catches more than a glimpse of her disapproval of the ways in which such parents conduct themselves towards their children. Indeed, she criticises both girls' and boys' education – the over-sheltering of girls as much as the over-indulgence of boys who are not subjected to discipline. The theory, generally accepted in her day, was that young men needed to experience everything in order to come through it all and gain strength in the process. Unfortunately, the fact that there were no limits to their activities only caused a great confusion of right and wrong in their minds, which led ultimately to secret misdemeanours and deceit. Although they were taught theoretically what was right, whenever they committed a wrong action their ill-doing was not punished, but often condoned, even praised, as we see in *Agnes Grey*, in the illustration of Tom Murray wanting to make sport with the unfortunate birds given him by Uncle Robson. As a result of such parental laxity, children learn to demand their own way at all times and, as they get older and this becomes more difficult to achieve, they manifest unrest by a lack of sticking power in whatever walk of life they take up – either no occupation and a life of idleness and debauch as with Anne's fictional character, Huntingdon, or a variety of unsuccessful lines as Anne had seen Branwell undertake. Branwell, being the only boy of the family, was his aunt's favourite, along with the baby, Anne, and, although he was brought up by her in true Methodist fashion, got away with far more than he should have done. His father also allowed him too much freedom, which he took advantage of in order to play with riotous village boys. As he grew older, he would go off drinking with the inmates of the nearby Black Bull and return home inebriated, when his father, who kept early hours, was in bed asleep. As a result of all this, he often told lies to his family to cover up his bad behaviour. Not only was Anne disappointed by her brother's attitude and his views on religion but Emily too, by 1836, was moving further and further away from her in a completely different direction, towards Pantheism. Anne became more introverted as a consequence, reticent to share her feelings, as is evident in her later autobiographical poem, *Self-Communion,* where she shows how she was compelled to act a part outwardly but inwardly was grieving at the growing separation between herself, her sister and brother. Indeed, Branwell, with his Calvinistic convictions, was moving towards such a crisis in his faith in that he even doubted the very existence of God and the validity of the Church teachings. Emily, at home with him, was probably subjected to his poetry and Angrian compositions and undoubtedly his negativity as regards his faith.[6] He felt he was damned, like Cowper:

> 'If there's no God, no Heaven, no Hell
> Thou within they grave must dwell –
> I left blackening in the storm –
> Both a banquet for the worm . . .
> And Hell's dread night must close my day!' [7]

Therefore, as far as he was concerned, it did not much signify what he did, for, as he was not one of the chosen elect, he could behave as he liked. This evidently offended Anne's susceptibility and strongly developed moral sense for she talks, in *Self-Communion,* of her dashed childhood hopes and fears and makes certain references to 'truth maintaining so little sway'. She goes on to state:

> 'How oft must sin and falsehood grieve
> A heart so ready to believe
> And willing to admire.'

This stanza probably alludes to her early disappointment in Branwell's conduct as a child, for one must not forget she spent a great deal of time with him, sharing many of his lessons and witnessing, at first hand, her father's excessive tolerance of his activities and indulgence towards him as his only son. As an adult, Branwell did consequently find it hard to retain any job and his weakness of character was evident in his drug-taking and drunkenness. During her time as a governess with her second employers, the Robinsons, when she saw Branwell succumb to seduction leading to his discharge, and during the following three years, when he existed at home on opium and alcohol, Anne became more and more convinced that lack of strong parental guidance could be held responsible for many such evils in society. Consequently, she resolved to instruct parents how to prevent their children from starting along such a wrong path. To do this with maximum impact, she used the only method of reaching the public open to her as a middle-class woman: that of publishing her ideas in her poetry and novels. In her first novel, although the subject is a serious one, she uses her humour to encourage the public to absorb her advice and instructions by entertaining them with the daily goings-on of a governess's life, most probably related to her own experience with the Inghams and the Robinsons. Indeed, one can note such a similarity to Anne's own posts as governess in *Agnes Grey,* where the first and much shorter part of the novel deals with Agnes's experiences with the young children of the Bloomfield family, reflecting Anne's short spell with the Inghams, progressing to the many more chapters which deal with the much longer time Agnes spent with the young Murray adults who were coming up to marriageable age, reflecting Anne's five years with the Robinsons. In *The Tenant,* Anne, through her sad witnessing of life at the Parsonage from 1845 on, has arrived at greater maturity of thought on the whole subject. She speaks at length of the disastrous consequences of such a lack of good parental guidance, voicing her objections against the inequality of male and female education and offering solutions through the voice of her fictional heroine:

> 'Well then, it must be that you think they are both weak and prone to err, and the slightest error, the merest shadow of pollution, will ruin the one, while the character of the other will be strengthened and embellished – his education properly finished by a little practical acquaintance with forbidden things . . . You would have us encourage our sons to prove all things by their own experience, while our daughters must not even profit by the experience of others. Now I would have both so to benefit by the experience of others, and the precepts of higher authority, that they should know beforehand to refuse the evil and choose the good, and require no experimental proofs to teach them the evil of transgression. I would not send a poor girl into the world unarmed against her foes, and ignorant of the snares that beset her path.' (TWH, p.27).

Chapter Two

Agnes Grey

In *Agnes Grey*, Anne uses a comparison of five fictitious marriages, only one of which is entirely happy or satisfactory, to lead us to believe that she is certainly not advocating marriage as the only means for a woman to reach fulfilment. Indeed, she is more concerned with offering guide-lines to her readers as to how to react when faced with similar problems to those illustrated in her text, be they marital or parental in nature. In Chapter One, scenes are taken from the marriage of Agnes's own parents, in the next four chapters from that of the Bloomfields, Agnes's first employers, in the next thirteen from that of her second employers, the Murrays, then, in the following two chapters from her pupil, Rosalie Murray's unhappy marriage to Sir Thomas Ashby, and finally, in the last chapter of the novel, briefly from Agnes's happy union with Edward Weston: 'a man of strong sense, firm faith, and ardent piety, but thoughtful and stern'. (AG, p.93).

Agnes Grey begins with a reminder of Anne's courageous resolve to tell her tale to a public she does not know, rather than to an intimate acquaintance, for in this way she reminds us she can remain unknown by using her pseudonym as an author: 'Shielded by my own obscurity, and by the lapse of years and a few fictitious names, I do not fear to venture, and I will candidly lay before the public what I would not disclose to the most intimate friend.' (p.15). Agnes then proceeds to narrate her tale in the first person and we are wafted into the Parsonage to meet the happy couple who are her parents. Anne paints a picture of a mother, who has married, beneath her social status, a relatively poor clergyman, but who is nevertheless happy with her lot. She does not hanker after the luxuries and the elegance of affluence to which her position as the daughter of rich gentlefolk might well have entitled her, had she followed their advice and married entirely for wealth rather than for love. She prefers life 'in a cottage with Richard Grey than in a palace with any other man in the world' (p.16). Anne's first picture of marriage is therefore quite idyllic, based, as it is, on mutual love and respect. Yet, even in the midst of all this bliss, she points out how difficulties can arise, even from within such a family situation. Indeed, Agnes's mother, although she does not 'regret past times' (p.18), frequently reminisces about them to her family, as apparently, Aunt Branwell also did to her young charges. The reader soon becomes aware that, through these stories of her former life of affluence, desires are being awakened in Mrs. Grey's children's breasts to experience more than their sheltered upbringing allows. In addition, her reminiscences are being misinterpreted by her husband and acting as a prompt to him to try and provide his wife with the kind of life-style to which she had formerly been accustomed. Unfortunately, such an approach spells danger for Richard Grey, who, forgetting the happiness of his marriage, becomes obsessed by his overriding wish to provide a better standard of living for his wife. Consequently, he makes very imprudent financial speculations to try and ease her burdens, which, through his imagination, have reached enormous proportions. Powerless to intervene, the reader watches as Rev. Richard Grey sets out on what he believes to be a well-meaning (but which turns out instead to be an entirely fool-hardy) course of action, which speedily leads him and his family to financial disaster. Anne portrays him as a man who does not fully understand how truly content his wife is in her present situation and who, through his lack of effective communication with her, commits, without much consultation, all his money to speculative action. His daughters as dutiful children accept his decision but his wife, portrayed as a thinking woman, fears the outcome of the speculation, and that he might well be extremely disappointed if things go badly. His motives are pure; he wants simply to better his wife's lot but unfortunately, in his attempt to accomplish this goal, his rash behaviour leads instead to near bankruptcy. Very quickly, life becomes much harder for this loving couple and their two daughters, now stripped of the former comforts from his investments that they had previously enjoyed. The wisdom of the mother is again evident when she suggests to her elder daughter, Mary, that, in order to pay for a few weeks at a watering hole for her father to aid him in his disappointment and illness, that she should get her pictures framed, along with some water-colour drawings she has already done and presented for sale: 'to some liberal picture-dealer, who has the sense to discern their merits' (p.25). This is a foretaste of how, in *The Tenant,* Helen Huntingdon will earn a living after having left her husband. Throughout these difficulties, Agnes's mother continues valiantly and cheerfully on just her husband's clergyman stipend, until, unfortunately, the worry of what he has done becomes too great for him to bear and causes his illness and premature death. The young girls, however, are never neglected and still cared for lovingly, not suffering from any lack of attention from their mother, even in the midst of her difficulties in caring for her sick husband.

As the younger daughter of the family, Agnes has been over-attentively cared for, through the excessive kindness (as opposed to indulgence) of her parents and sister. This has almost succeeded in rendering her 'too helpless and dependent, too unfit for buffeting with the cares and turmoils of life' (p.17). Even when the afore-mentioned financial disaster strikes, Agnes is discouraged from helping out at home and has to use great strength of character and all her will-power to persuade her parents and her elder sister to allow her to take up a post as governess. This reminds us of Anne Brontë's own background where she, also the baby of the family, had difficulty in persuading her family, most of all Charlotte and her father, of her competence to take up a post as governess. Indeed, Agnes had to emphasise her great enthusiasm, remarking 'and I should like it so much – I am so fond of children'. (p.26) which possibly echoes Anne's own words said in order to persuade her family to allow her to work as a governess. Agnes's motives are shown to be pure and prayerful, as were most probably Anne Brontë's, in her desire to alleviate her family's financial situation. Yet, one cannot ignore that, coupled with this desire to help her parents, there is a very strong desire, on her part, to experience a new life and a chance to exercise her unused faculties. The reasons Agnes gives, considering Anne's normal restraint and usual economy of language, cover quite a lot of ground. Her long explanation as to why she wants to become a governess, therefore, assumes some importance as a possibly true statement. Agnes says:

> 'How delightful it would be to be a governess! To go out into the world; to enter into a new life; to act for myself; to exercise my unused faculties; to try my unknown powers; to earn my own maintenance, and something to comfort and help my father, mother, and sister, besides exonerating them from the provision of my food and clothing; to show papa what his little Agnes could do; to convince mamma and Mary that I was not quite the helpless, thoughtless being they supposed' (pp.27/8).

As the phrases flow from Anne's pen, we positively feel the intensity of her feelings in the reasons she provides and we become aware that these are thoughts she might well have experienced, wanting, as she did, to go out into the world to begin her first post as governess to the Inghams, like Agnes, at the tender age of nineteen years. The reader watches Agnes deal with her problems through her reliance on prayer and a core set of values. This is very apparent when the moment arrives for her to take up her post and leave her family home. The way in which she simply but persistently prays for God's blessings on her family, as she journeys away from them for the very first time in her life, is sincerely touching. Agnes's upbringing, although far too lenient as the baby of the family, has prepared her for coping in most situations, and her mother is seen to use similar techniques of instruction to those Anne probably experienced in her infancy at the hands of her aunt, which involved living by example rather than by oral command, or doing as she did rather than as she said. Eventually, Agnes gets her way and begins her first post as governess to the three children of the Bloomfields at Wellwood House: Tom (seven years old), Mary Ann (six years old), and Fanny (nearly four years old). She recognises the fact that her mother's and sister's 'protecting care' means that 'many a girl of fifteen or under, was gifted with a more womanly address, and a greater ease and self-possession' (p.34) than she felt she had. In stating this, Anne is drawing our attention to the ills of over-sheltering young girls.

Through another of Anne's illustrations, the reader perceives that no mother's teaching is infallible, for, although Agnes has been well briefed by her mother, on arrival, at the Bloomfield's house, she finds, to her great disappointment, that her role and her treatment by Mrs. Bloomfield are certainly different from what she has been led to expect. Her new charges are very badly behaved and entirely bereft of parental interest or discipline. Agnes is also shocked at Mrs. Bloomfield's distinctly condescending attitude towards herself and finds her 'cold, grave, and forbidding' (p.43). Yet, as she has been brought up to do, she manages to rally quickly and, as regards the children, she resolves 'to work a reformation' in them (p.39) and to try to win their affection so as to point out to them the error of their ways. Instead of giving up, Agnes shows the way in which her character has been formed during her childhood and determines to deal with the situation by showing love and giving of her best to succeed. Her mother has brought her up to be self-controlled in her utterances, neither a word too much nor too little, and, therefore, she manages to refrain from mentioning to the pampered and ostensibly over-doting Mrs. Bloomfield the full extent of her children's faults. By always concentrating on the positive rather than on the negative, Agnes struggles on valiantly to achieve her goals. Little Fanny is given a splendid character, as indeed is her brother, Tom, by Mrs. Bloomfield, and being nearly four years of age is allowed to learn the alphabet and be promoted to the school-room, where much mischief occurs. Agnes learns very quickly what the reality of the situation is, however, in her initial dealings with Tom, where she experiences for herself how imperiously he acts towards her and also how undisciplined he is, striking his sister at will 'to keep her in order' (p.39). She learns of his bad-nature on the very first day, when he tells her how he means to roast alive the next bird he manages to entrap. In response, Agnes reveals a method of dealing with such boastful statements, which appears a much wiser method than simply telling him how wicked such an action would be. She teaches him, instead, where wicked people go if they indulge in such bad activities, telling him that he will go there too if 'you don't leave off torturing innocent birds' (p.41). His response is that his father thoroughly approves of his actions, and that he is only doing what his father did as a boy. The previous summer, his Uncle Robson had praised him too as a 'fine boy' (p.41) when he had pulled off the legs and wings of a nest of young sparrows. He also reveals that his mother does not mind what he does to 'naughty sparrows and mice and rats' (p.42). Agnes's way of dealing with all this rather disturbing information, which illustrates, in no mean terms, the contrast with his mother's portrayal of him as a 'generous, noble spirit' (p.42), is to listen to him intently and to let him chatter on in order to better understand his motives. Evidently, her hope is to win his affection and gradually show him the error of his ways. We, the readers, can make our own conclusions as to how indulgently his parents have treated him, the only boy of the family, letting him do exactly as he likes and stay up until 8 pm, much later than his sister, Mary Ann, whose bed-time is at 7 pm. Indeed, we learn from a letter sent by Anne's sister, Charlotte, to Ellen Nussy on 15 April 1839, what Anne herself had to suffer during her first appointment as a governess, and also of her actual methods of teaching two of the Ingham children at Blake Hall, the counterparts of the three Bloomfield children. Charlotte says of Anne in her letter: 'The little monkies are excessively indulged and she is not empowered to inflict any punishment. She is requested when they misbehave themselves to inform their Mamma – which she says is utterly out of the question as in that case she might be making complaints from morning till night – So she alternatively scolds, coaxes and threatens – sticks to her first word and gets on as well as she can.'

Agnes finds her pupils 'very backward indeed' (p.45), for, although Tom is indeed bright, Mary Ann can scarcely read a word. Agnes's method of overcoming the carelessness and inattention she meets in the children is to show them patience. We see what a long way she has to go, for they refuse to do anything she wants to do and insist on her following their every desire. 'No arguments, commands, or entreaties' (p.45) work on them. Indeed, their actions cause her constant reproofs from Mr. Bloomfield, who, without even bothering to introduce himself to her, scolds her for not controlling the children better: 'Let me request that in future you will keep them decent at least!' Agnes is surprised at his lack of civility to her, a perfect stranger.

From the first, Agnes tries to establish the pattern of her teaching days, which bears resemblance to John Locke's programme of education with its emphasis on physical activities. There are lessons in the mornings, recreation before luncheon at 1 pm, more lessons in the afternoon and then more recreation before tea in the school-room and getting Mary Ann ready to join her parents for dessert in the dining room. Agnes's efforts are more often than not made in vain for her pupils have 'no more notion of obedience than a wild unbroken colt' (p.49). Neither 'fear of anger' nor 'desire of approbation' have any effect on them. She would have liked to suggest 'a few sound boxes on the ear' or 'a good birch rod' but, as she has to correct the children's waywardness and wilful misbehaviour without any physical discipline, she is unable to adopt such measures and consequently all her efforts to reprove them without physical punishment meet with failure. Such a method of punishment would, in any case, have been denied her, as she is later informed by Betty, the nurse, who has been dismissed because she could not control her impulses to correct the children by slapping them. Betty fails to understand how Agnes can manage to show such forbearance. Yet, Agnes decides that her only weapons will have to be 'patience, firmness and perseverance' (p.50). She insists that the children always finish any short task she sets them taking due care never to make any rash claims which she cannot substantiate or execute. This allows her always to carry out 'the threats and promises she has made to the children' (p.51) and to keep their trust. Her claim is that no child would ever again take her at her word if she were to compromise herself in that way and would, as a result, increase rather than decrease in unruliness. She makes a huge distinction between their good and bad conduct, showing them great kindness, but never indulgence, and being very obliging when they behave tolerably well and being sorrowful, rather than angry, whenever they do wrong. She treats their naughtiness by giving them 'penitential hymns' to recite and rewards their comparatively good behaviour with 'cheerful ones'. Indeed, she totally defuses each difficult situation, dealing with the problem by teaching the child to compose hymns and prayers, to suggest a seeming desire on the child's behalf to be forgiven for any wrongs committed. Therefore, she does not leave it entirely up to the child to apologize but instead helps him along gently, showing him how to present his excuses sincerely but without losing too much face. Her method incorporates the idea of giving 'every kind of instruction . . . by entertaining discourse – apparently with no other object than their present amusement in view' (p.51). For these difficult tasks, she constantly implores divine assistance, for the children often provoke her to feel ill-tempered and irritable – feelings usually quite

difficult to control. Sometimes, she is exhausted by the physical
nature of the work such as having to hold down a large child of seven
years and even having to force him to write an extra line for writing so
badly. Apart from Tom's obstinacy, she has difficulties with Mary Ann
and informs the reader that all would have been better served if she
'had passed it over as a matter of no consequence' instead of meeting
the problem head-on. Agnes finds it difficult to comprehend how
'neglect and disgrace' (p.54) do not seem to be the most dreadful
punishments for a child as they certainly would have been to her.
Mary Ann would simply ignore such threats and scream to get her
mother involved, so that Miss Grey would be in trouble. Fanny too
proved intractable and Agnes soon gets blamed for this, by the
Bloomfields, whose use of underhand innuendo within her hearing
makes her very aware of their disapproval of her methods. Agnes
manages to control herself from making an outburst in return,
keeping her feelings secret from them, but not from us, reminiscent of
Anne's own attitude to any suffering she endured, which she often
translated into poetry. Agnes continues to do her best to 'subdue every
resentful impulse' and 'to struggle on with unremitting firmness and
integrity' (p.59) to fulfil her purpose of humanizing the children.
Agnes recognizes, and therefore her readers do too, how necessary it is
to make the children wiser and more manageable before they get any
older, for 'a child of nine or ten as frantic and ungovernable as these at
six and seven would be a maniac' (p.59). She perseveres in this
nightmarish post not only to help her parents financially but also to
justify to herself that she is 'competent to undertake the charge' and
to do it 'honourably to the end' (p.60).

On one occasion, not just one but all three of the Bloomfield
children decide to be naughty and, against her wishes, they rush out of
the house into the snowy gardens. It all begins with Fanny spitting
into Agnes's work-bag and then proceeding, on Tom's command, to
throw it into the fire. While Agnes is rushing to rescue it, Mary Ann
prepares to throw her 'precious desk, containing my letters and
papers, my small amount of cash, and all my valuables' (p.64) out of
the third storey window. On rescuing her desk, she sees them rush out
of the house and plunge into the snow outside, shouting and
screaming wildly. Mr. Bloomfield, unfortunately, witnesses their exit
and roars at them to come back into the house. He seems to gloat over
her failure to get the children to obey her. Indeed, everything is made
worse by the fact that, once he intervenes with his threat of 'Come in
with you, you filthy brats or I'll horsewhip you every one!', the
children instantly obey him and rush indoors. He remains, however,
incapable of recognising that his authority comes from his menacing
tone and from the fact that he is their father and able to punish them

in any way he wishes. His urging her to 'see them made decent, for
Heaven's sake!' highlights not only his lack of respect for the
governess but also his complete lack of interest in his children. To him
they are merely symbols of his social status and, according to the
Victorian maxim, should only be seen and not heard. As long as
society is not offended by them in any way and they are always
presentable and 'decently' dressed, (this word 'decent' keeps
recurring in his speech), they are acceptable to his life-style. He sees
no need to show them any love or respect, but rather prefers to shelve
his responsibility for them onto the shoulders of a paid governess,
whose job it is to prevent them from interfering with his life-style.
Here Agnes makes us aware of how bad the relationship between
father and children really is. However, she does not lack courage
responding honestly to his gloating over his success, by saying rather
pointedly: 'Yes . . . when *you* speak they respond.' (my italics). At this
point, the grandmother also intervenes and shows her true colours,
asking if Agnes can be 'a proper person'. Up to this point in time, Mrs.
Bloomfield Senior has adopted a kind and attentive attitude towards
Agnes, who, finding it difficult to cope without any of the loving
protection to which she was accustomed in her own home, has
responded to her and been thoroughly taken in by her false approach.
Agnes learns through bitter experience how 'hypocritical and
insincere, a flatterer, and a spy upon my words and deeds' (p.66) the
grandmother really was. Anne's dislike of double standards and deceit
comes up again and again and is evidently something very alien to her
nature, as is apparent when she is subjected to Branwell's lying
words. Anne juxtaposes her wry humour here against the gravity of
the situation, to highlight more clearly the hypocrisy of the way in
which the elderly lady acts. Agnes cannot be false in return and
describes the theatrical, almost farcical, gestures reminiscent of
Molière's *Tartuffe,* which accompany the grandmother's words, when
she recounts to Agnes her pious resignation to life: 'But there's one
remedy for all, my dear, and that's resignation' *(a toss of the head),*
'resignation to the will of Heaven!' (an uplifting of the hands and
eyes) . . . 'I'm one of the pious ones, Miss Grey!' (a very significant nod
and toss) . . . 'and I glory in it!' (an emphatic clasping of the hands and
shaking of the head). After this dramatic display culminating in
'several texts of scripture, misquoted or misapplied', and many
ludicrous religious exclamations Agnes is left, declining to repeat any
more of the grandmother's expressions, and hoping against hope that
'she was rather weak than wicked' (pp.66/67/68).

    Another illustration, taken from the Bloomfields' relationship, also
proves enlightening and typifies many of the child-rearing problems
which exist in modern times. Once again, we see how a lack of

communication between a man and his wife can introduce discontent
and bring about a marital break-down which, in the Bloomfield's case,
is seen to be a spiritual and mental growing apart from each other,
rather than a physical separation. Anne reveals to the reader through
Agnes a rather upsetting scene which takes place at table in the
Bloomfields' household, where Agnes is shocked at the bad relations
which exist between the married couple. Mr. Bloomfield, before
Agnes's very eyes, openly blames his wife for mis-management of the
household staff and in particular chides her for allowing 'the savages'
(p.45) in the kitchen to ruin both his beef and his mutton. He
continues to rant on about his wife's not having chosen a particular
fish for his evening meal. Agnes can only look on, powerless to
intervene, at the hateful scene in which Mr. Bloomfield exhibits his
spoilt childish attitude and his utter indifference for the feelings of
those present, even for those of his wife and gathered children, or for
those of a relative stranger to his household, the new governess. The
darkness of the situation is contrasted with the lightness of Anne's
humorous intervention voiced by Agnes who remarks that, although
very annoyed by the state of the meat, 'the gentleman managed to cut
himself some delicate slices, part of which he ate in silence' (p.47).
Many other examples in the novel reveal a similar lack of respect for
the marriage partner and show the reader how this can be one of the
main causes of friction in a household. The bad behaviour of children
who witness this parental division day in day out, becomes easier to
understand. Yet, even here, Anne's thoughts on what ought to be done
remain unspoken and are implicit in her illustrations. The reader is
presented with the facts of the case through the first person narrative
of Agnes and left to reach his own conclusions. No instructions are
directly imparted and the reader is urged only indirectly to reflect and
to reach a judgment as to how to react when presented with similar
circumstances in life.

For the most part, as already stated, Agnes emphasises the fun of
what she is teaching, seeming to have no other object in view than the
amusement of her charges. Yet, to the reader, who can admire this
intelligent, far-seeing approach, it is evident that she is using fun with
a particular goal in mind, i.e. to point children through it towards
better behaviour and an acceptance of certain values. Agnes's
unremitting patience and perseverance are an inspiration to the
reader. However, constant success on her part could have proved
nauseating to the reader and Anne, a master of entertaining, senses
this and allows her protagonist to fail several times to get the results
she wants, even after exerting her most strenuous efforts. Through
these failures, Anne shows us how to proceed, for she portrays an
Agnes whose dogged determination makes her persevere against all

odds. She remains resolute that she will not give up what she has already managed to achieve up to that point, simply to gain a temporary peace. She leads us to understand that this would only put back to zero all her good efforts. Indeed, we become increasingly aware, on watching Agnes chase round after her charges, constantly keeping an eye on their activities and unselfishly sticking firm to the programme of the day, that the most necessary qualities for anyone who looks after children are not only spiritual, mental and physical strength, but especially great wisdom. An example of the latter can be seen when Agnes accepts misdemeanours of *little* consequence without too much of a reaction, rather than risk the outright rebellion and obstinacy of a child. Indeed, it seems to be her policy that she enforces discipline only when it is absolutely necessary.

Even though the parents themselves are totally unwilling to put themselves out to form any relationship with their children, they show resentment at Agnes's ability to cajole, control and even interest them. As they have not been party to any code of values in their own infancy, evident from the deceitful approach of the parents and the grandmother towards Agnes, they find it incomprehensible that this strictly programmed way of life should be at all attractive to their children. Their lack of comprehension allows them to level criticism and innuendo at Agnes, which she bears remarkably well. We see her, sometimes with great difficulty, subdue any 'resentful impulse' (p.59) and we admire her self-control. Anne shows us an example of this when Mrs. Bloomfield, in a case of parental complicity of the worst kind, joins with her husband in the use of innuendo against Agnes and complains that the children had 'deteriorated of late' in order to hurt her and undermine the authority the governess had gained up to that point. Instead of making open accusations against her, Mrs. Bloomfield assumes this more deceitful approach, never permitting any blame to be attached to herself for her children's faults. Agnes is horrified to find that Mrs. Bloomfield's portrait of her daughter, Fanny, as being gentle and honest, is utterly fallacious. The little girl is full of 'falsehood and deception' (p.58), unfortunately, but very understandably, like her parents and her grandmother. However, Agnes is not entirely a free agent or able to defend herself as she might have liked against their verbal attacks, for her code of behaviour compels her to ignore such base remarks and thereby retain her post. She resolves instead to use 'unremitting firmness and integrity' (p.59) in order to render the children 'more humanized.' Her firmness of purpose is combined with an amazing patience and forgiving spirit, for, when she is refused her correct amount of holidays after a very long term's work, she does not grumble. Instead, she lives out, by example, the Christian value of loving one's neighbour as oneself, accepting completely Mrs. Bloomfield's rather dubious explanation and even supporting her employer by telling her that she was 'justified in not allowing her a full vacation as she felt she had not perhaps completed a full term of work'. Conveniently, as is often the case, the reader is presented with a statement, as here, which offers both sides of the argument, enabling him to reach his own conclusions!

Agnes not only suffers at the hands of the parents but also of the servants when they refuse to clear up after the children at her request. Governesses, in Victorian times, often laboured under conditions in which they were looked down on, maligned and even badly treated by both employers and servants, who had difficulty in placing them in the class structure, for they felt they belonged to neither class. Even earlier in the late eighteenth century, we see evidence of this attitude prevailing in Mary Wollstonecraft's *Education of Daughters*. In her section entitled, *Unfortunate Situation of Females, Fashionably Educated and Left without a Fortune*, Wollstonecraft describes a governess as being 'Above the servants, yet considered by them as a spy, and ever reminded of her inferiority when in conversation with the superiors'. On one occasion, Agnes is humiliated by Tom, one of her charges, when he refuses to do his share of tidying up. The servants, as usual, remain uncooperative, only to obey Tom's mother instantly when she makes a similar request. The injustice of the situation becomes even more apparent when Tom, after he has again refused even to obey his mother's request to help tidy up, is still allowed by her to have his supper. Consequently, this total lack of discipline of the child and sheer indulgence by his mother allows Tom to vaunt his superiority over his governess. His mother by her action undermines not only any authority Agnes might have won up to this point but also any bargaining power she might have held over the naughty child.

Honesty is one of Agnes's main qualities and pervades her approach to teaching the children in her charge. She feels incapable of acting out a part with parents and grandparents even to better her situation. She always reveals her true feelings and alters her manner according to her emotions, so making what she is feeling very obvious to the recipient. There is never any pretence, for she refuses to 'toady' to her employer just to gain certain benefits. In the end, this great ability of hers always to be herself and maintain her integrity gains the respect of the children who realise that whatever she says to them is sincere and that her word can always be trusted. Sometimes, when Agnes is unable to respond to outright rudeness for, amongst other reasons, fear of losing her job, her very human irritation surfaces as she fails to hide her emotions. One afternoon in spring, when all the children are miraculously playing happily together, Mr. Bloomfield enters the school-room. Unable to find anything to complain about other than that the children are playing quietly on the carpet with broken eggshells, he chides Agnes rudely for this and rushes out saying that it all puts him past his patience and calling his children 'you little devils' (p.71). Agnes, unusually for her, shows her annoyance by responding under her breath, muttering: It puts me quite past my patience too!' (p.72). However, even in her anger, she manages to control any further outburst, venting all unspent wrath instead on poking the fire over-vehemently.

As already mentioned, Agnes, as a mere governess and paid employee, is not allowed by the parents to correct the children's misbehaviour by physical means. As she continues in her post, she finds, to add to her difficulty, that the children scorn any authority which has no terrors to back it up (p.82). Her attempts at instilling good values are often mocked by an interesting succession of different relatives, such as the children's uncle, Mr. Robson, who during their visits to Wellwood, each present her with a different brand of problems. This portrait of Uncle Robson, whom Anne calls lofty-minded and manly, 'the scorner of the female sex' who 'was not above the foppery of stays' to compress his waist, reveals the odds against which Agnes was working and is presented in delightfully tongue-in-cheek fashion, which contrasts greatly with the horror of the situation. Mr. Robson encourages the children in their bad behaviour and even in drunkenness, which passes completely unopposed by the children's father, who seems to have a strong liking himself for a plentiful supply of gin and water and therefore sees no wrong in encouraging his young son to follow in his footsteps. He also urges Mary Ann to dwell on her personal appearance by encouraging her to become even more affected, in direct opposition to Agnes's hopes to get her to focus on the cultivation of her mind and manners. He laughs at the children's faults, which Agnes suggests is perhaps not the best way to proceed! He treats his dogs so badly that even Agnes claims she would have gladly parted with a sovereign to see them bite him in return. Indeed, Uncle Robson is a very bad influence on the children, encouraging them to show cruelty to animals and birds as he does, and openly opposing Agnes's attempts to introduce them to justice and humanity. A forceful illustration of this is given in the episode of the five birds in a nest which Uncle Robson gives to Tom as 'a rare sport' for him. Agnes, fearful for the fate of the birds at Tom's torturing hands, cannot bear to stand by and watch such cruelty, so she tells him that, if he does not return them at once to the place from which they were originally collected, she will kill them herself to prevent any prolonged suffering on their part. On meeting Tom's absolute refusal to comply with her request, Agnes takes a 'large flat stone' and drops it on the 'intended victims' crushing them flat beneath it. This is similar to Mary Wollstonecraft's fictitious character, Mrs. Mason, in her *Original Stories,* where Mrs. Mason 'crushes the head of a fallen lark with her foot rather than see it suffer'.[8] Both these women, Mrs. Mason and Agnes are seen to act in a rational manner. Rather than allow the birds to suffer, they take action. Indeed, Jane Moore talks of how Mary Wollstonecraft created a woman who 'applies discipline and reason to her daily duties and does so independently of men' (p.29), which, in my opinion could also be a description of what Anne is advocating in this example. We see Tom reacting violently to Agnes's action even to the point of trying to kick her. Yet, instead of reprimanding his nephew for his incredibly rude behaviour in swearing and kicking out at his governess, Uncle Robson praises his 'spunk' saying that he is 'a noble little scoundrel . . . beyond petticoat government already.' He goes on to say: 'By God! he defies mother, granny, governess, and all!' and exalts in his actions as if these are attributes in his nephew of which he should be really proud. This reveals much of what Anne is trying to point out in the male attitude to females, prevalent at the time, especially to those paid subordinates with whom the master comes into contact. Through this illustration she reveals what must happen to man if, from childhood, he is allowed to do whatever he likes, growing up, as has Uncle Robson, never to be quelled and constantly issuing forth rudeness and incivility in truly arrogant style. Anne seems, once again, to be making excuses for the child, saying that it is not his fault if, by the time he reaches manhood, he has been given no code of values other than his own selfishness on which to base his behaviour.

Eventually, and not surprisingly, Agnes is dismissed from this first post, as had been Anne from hers with the Inghams, and Wollstonecraft, in August 1787, from her post as governess to Lady Kingsborough's children. On her return home, we see Agnes benefit greatly from the sympathy and kindness of her parents. In no way do they triumph over her failure or reprove her for losing her situation. They also refuse to take the much needed money she presses on them. At the Parsonage, the loving relationship between father and daughter is resumed with Agnes cheering her sick parent by her attempts 'to amuse him with singing his favourite songs'. His constant worries over what will become of his wife and daughters when he dies, 'poor penniless things' as he calls them, are countered by his wife and daughters. Indeed, the idea, put forward by his wife 'that it's no matter whether they get married or not, we can devise a thousand honest ways of making a livelihood' (pp.86/7) strongly reflects Anne's attitude that marriage is not the only possible outcome in life for a woman. This remark also reflects the population distribution of the Victorian age, for, written as the novel is in 1846-47, just prior to the Census of 1851, women did indeed far outnumber men. As a result, the difficulty of finding a husband must have been uppermost in young women's and mothers' hearts and minds. Agnes's mother's down-to-earth attitude mirrors Anne's, especially with the emphasis on 'honest ways' of earning a living. The ensuing discussion on the difficulties Agnes has faced when working for the Bloomfields helps her to gain valuable advice from her mother as on how she herself had coped with bringing up her two little girls, who were by no means 'perfect angels'. Her advice is clear and effective, simply not to spoil them.

Agnes remains firm in her desire to try again as a governess and her mother urges her not to minimise the talents she has which 'are not such as every poor clergyman's daughter possesses'. This encouragement helps her to decide not to stay at home and gives her enough confidence to try her luck once again. To do so, she decides to analyse the qualities she might need to overcome similar difficulties in the future, if she were ever again to be the governess of unruly children and unhappy parents. She comes up with 'unshaken firmness, devoted diligence, unwearied perseverance, unceasing care' (p.83) as being the ingredients necessary for success. So, she resolves to seek another post where, once again, she can put her talents into practice. Her mother shows great interest in her daughter's ambitions, guiding her and giving her particularly sound advice on how to place an advertisement which will show off to the full her qualifications of 'Music, singing, drawing, French, Latin and German' (p.90), evidently considered as more than adequate requirements to gain a post in education in Victorian England. The mother, in the opinion she offers her daughter, reveals her own upbringing in the home of a gentleman for she states a preference for Agnes to find a post in the home of 'some genuine, thorough-bred gentleman; for such are far more likely [she felt] to treat you with proper respect and consideration, than those purse-proud tradespeople and arrogant upstarts' (p.90). However, she does manage to say that there is some good and bad in all classes, allowing some extenuating circumstances for her remarks. The contrast between Agnes's mother's reflections on the gentry and Agnes's experiences in their homes is highlighted by Anne's technique of revealing what is expected to happen in advance of its happening. Here, her mother is convinced that, if Agnes can find a post in such a household, she will be treated much better than in her previous engagement, when the reality proves entirely different. In any case, Agnes receives only two replies to her advertisement but, aided by her mother, manages to attain her desired £50 salary, two months' holiday and also a post where she can teach older children. Her new employers, the Murrays, insist on a governess of 'next to unimpeachable morality, a mild and cheerful temper and obliging disposition' (p.91). Would we not all like to know our children were being educated by such a person? Agnes, intensely worried by her father's health situation and her mother's lack of comfort, determines to overcome the apprehension she feels, about the way this new family would treat her and to accept the post.

So, after a brief restful interlude at the Parsonage, in Chapter 6, Agnes leaves home to teach, having progressed from her work with the young Bloomfields to this new adventure of teaching older children. In the Murray family, her youngest pupil, Charles, is ten years old, followed by John, eleven years of age. However, these two young lads are, fortunately for her, sent off to school shortly after her arrival. Agnes is able to concentrate her efforts on her two remaining charges, Rosalie, sixteen years of age, and Matilda, fourteen years of age.

Although reassured by her mother before her departure, Agnes's secret fears are indeed realized on 31 January on reaching the Murrays' home, Horton Lodge, near O-, about 70 miles from her village – no mean distance in those days. After a terrible journey in the snow, she is taken into the school-room, where she meets her pupils. Her first impression of Rosalie is of a girl who 'was trifling over a piece of canvas and a basket of German wools'. Plain sewing would certainly not have been in order here in this household, as fancy needlework and Berlin wools were thought to make a much more fashionable impression.[9] Anne's use of 'trifling' suggests that, from the first glimpse of Rosalie, Agnes was aware that the girl was interested solely in making an impression on others rather than on acquiring the skill of more intricate needlework. After accepting tea, Agnes is taken by Matilda to a 'small but tolerably comfortable room' (p.96). So far, so good, but, on noticing that her luggage had still not arrived, she is compelled to venture downstairs and to ask a lady's maid for assistance, or such as she thinks the extremely well-dressed female she meets en route to be. The house-maid, as she turns out to be, shows Agnes no respect and only reluctantly agrees to engage the services of a fellow manservant to bring her luggage to her room. Through this illustration we are reminded of Anne's own inferiority complex regarding her own rather plain attire, which might well, on her visits, have been intensified by the appearance of a maid, 'a well-dressed female' in better clothes than herself. This also reflects the self-consciousness at her extremely plain attire, which she might well have felt, when she and Charlotte attended the London Opera with

Charlotte's publisher, George Smith, and his fashionably dressed sisters. Much was evidently based on appearances and wealth in Victorian times. How difficult it must have been for a respectable, well-educated but poor gentlewoman, such as Anne and her fictional counterpart, to be accepted for what they were, rather than for their appearance.

Nor was she welcomed on that first day by her employer, Mrs. Murray, 'a handsome dashing lady of forty, who required neither rouge nor padding to add to her charms' (p.100) . However, Mrs. Murray does condescend to visit her briefly the following day, to talk to her curtly about the weather and then promptly to disappear. Agnes, voicing Anne's sense of humour, says, 'she honoured me with a visit, just as my mother might step into the kitchen to see a new servant girl (p.101). She adds, however, rather smugly, the quip that her mother would have seen the girl immediately after her arrival. Once again, we see Anne juxtaposing two ways of greeting a new person to the household, comparing Mrs. Murray's treatment of Agnes, who, although a paid employee, was a gentlewoman like herself, with Agnes's mother's respectful treatment of an uneducated kitchen maid, in order to focus the reader's attention on the injustice of the comparison. More irony follows with Mrs. Murray petting her youngest child, Charles, even though, as Agnes remarks, he 'had just been wiping his mouth and hands on her gown, after indulging in some savoury morsel from the housekeeper's stores'. Mrs. Murray then proceeds to tell Agnes what 'a sweet, good boy he was'. Agnes is not fooled and gives us her thoughts on this doting attitude of Mrs. Murray by adding 'I alone thought otherwise' (p.101). Mr. Murray, true to the form that Agnes will observe in him as her post progresses, does not manage to make any appearance before her at all, but occasionally Agnes meets him in the house or hears his loud laugh and his 'swearing and blaspheming against the footman, groom, coachman, or some other hapless dependent' (p.100), a habit which, to Agnes's horror, his younger daughter, Matilda, duly adopts! Mrs. Murray later elaborates to Agnes on her wishes for her girls' education, stating that she wants them rendered 'as superficially attractive as they could possibly be made.' Again, this emphasis on outward appearance and presentation rather than on inner worth for as long as Victorian society perceived them to be finished products, their inner beings were considered of no importance whatsoever. Agnes is given a pretty impossible task to complete for she is told she must 'study and strive to amuse and oblige, instruct, refine and polish, with the least possible exertion on their part and no exercise of authority' (p.102) on her part. Mrs. Murray's requests are similar for her boys' education. However, she does add Latin and Valpy's *Delectus* to her list and again reiterates that Agnes must teach them 'without trouble to themselves' (p.102). Ostensibly, Mrs. Murray thus claims to be solicitous for the comfort and happiness of her children but can never once lower herself to mention Agnes's comfort except to tell her to 'keep her temper and be mild and patient throughout'. Anne emphasises, through this illustration, the double standards of her day where, rather hypocritically, Mrs. Murray advocates a 'meek and quiet spirit' (p.102) to which she feels Agnes, as a clergyman's daughter, should easily be able to find reference in the Bible, although she herself, as Anne wryly allows her to say, has no idea where such a reference can be found! Another example of this love of outward show can be seen in Agnes's ironic remark about how 'Mr. and Mrs. Murray generally thought it sufficient to show themselves at church once in the course of the day' (p.112).

At the start of this second post, Agnes's eldest charge, Rosalie Murray, was sixteen years of age and 'a decidedly pretty girl' although rather vain and empty-headed. Indeed her faults are listed as many although 'there was so much of what was pleasing and prepossessing in herself' (p.104). Agnes again points out the way Rosalie has been taught as being to blame, rather than its being the young lady's disposition and indicates that it is the lack of guidance and control which are responsible for her state. From infancy she had been allowed 'to tyrannize over horses, governesses, and servants; she had not been taught to moderate her desires, to control her temper or bridle her will, or to sacrifice her own pleasure for the good of others' and here's the nub of it 'from constant indulgence and habitual scorn of reason, she was often testy and capricious; her mind had never been cultivated', and she had had fostered in her a love of display which induced her only to apply herself to 'showy accomplishments' such as 'French, German, music, singing, dancing, fancy-work, and a little drawing' (p.105). Evidently, left to her own devices, with no useful occupation, yet provided with everything money could buy, including the showiest tutors, Rosalie Murray had found no incentive to improve her mind. When Agnes arrived, Rosalie's relationship with her parents is practically non-existent on a deeper level, so, naturally, having no-one to guide her, all her thoughts centre on herself and her own comfort. Her mother supported her doing anything she liked, as long as it led ultimately to her becoming more attractive in the marriage market. Matilda is described as 'a veritable hoyden' (p.106), who cares little about her appearance or about the cultivation of her mind. She 'slurred over' the tasks set her, but any remonstration on Agnes's part caused her mother to intervene quite reprehensibly. This grieves Agnes, who sees herself responsible for 'cultivating her understanding, reforming her manners, and aiding her to acquire these ornamental attainments, which, unlike her sister, she despised as much as the rest' (p.108). Her mother is incapable of understanding how nothing can be taught her daughters without some little exertion on their part too, and cannot think how Matilda picks up her unladylike tricks. We, the readers, are quite aware how this has come about, for Matilda unfolds readily to Miss Grey, as she calls Agnes, the persons responsible for her swearing and rough habits. Not surprisingly, they turn out to be her father and the coachman: 'I learnt it all from him; and may be a bit from the coachman' (p.109). Completely uninterested by any of her lessons, she is only in good humour when they are over. However, Agnes persists in her aim to overcome such faults and resolves to turn her into a young lady of reformed manners and ornamental attainments by always speaking the truth and steadily helping her to profess good principles. Agnes's last ploy is to endeavour 'to make inclination bow to duty' (p.104) and to make her charges aware that they cannot always do what they want to do until they have carried out certain tasks or duties. This might well be an attitude which Anne absorbed from her reading of Hannah More's *Coelebs in search of a wife,* where it is accentuated in the Stanley family's education. Even on arrival, Agnes feels that John, the elder Murray boy, might have been a decent lad, instead of a young tyrant, had he received a more disciplined and work-orientated educational programme. This constant emphasis by Anne on how children are indeed helped or marred by their parents reveals the intensity of her feelings on this issue. Fortunately, John and his younger brother, Charles, soon go away to school, for Agnes has become aware that Charles, in distinct contrast to the representation his mother has made of him, is only 'active in doing mischief and in malicious wantonness to hurt others'.

The lack of consideration shown by the youngsters towards their governess and their complete disregard for her comforts is duplicated by the servants who often neglect Agnes and despise her requests, even though, in direct contrast to what they do for her, she often stands up for them against the 'the tyranny and injustice of their young masters and mistresses' (p.115). Agnes resolves to live out her faith by 'turning the other cheek'. Instead of complaining, she chides herself for her lack of Christian humility even when she feels rather degraded by such treatment. However, with time and patience, her plan begins to work, although until then she has to bear a great deal from her charges.

Once her male pupils go away to school, Agnes begins to gain esteem in the eyes of Rosalie and Matilda, and reports what she has heard about herself to show the readers the change in attitude which is beginning to take place in Rosalie and Matilda: 'Miss Grey was a queer creature; she never flattered, and did not praise them half enough: but whenever she did speak favourably of them, or anything belonging to them, they could be quite sure her approbation was sincere' (p.116). The picture Anne paints here of Agnes is of a caring governess who uses plain-spoken honesty to deal fairly with her charges. Her approbation for her fictional creation who is described as being 'someone so different from the girls' mamma' yet who could still be 'very agreeable and amusing sometimes, in her way', even though the girls felt that she held some very 'tiresome opinions' and 'had a strange reverence for matters connected with religion, and an unaccountable liking to good people' (p.116), resembles in many ways the compassionate, fair and forthright lady who had brought her up, her Aunt Branwell.

The novel skims over the next two years leading to the 'coming out' of Miss Murray at eighteen years of age into the fashionable world of society. By now the relationship between governess and charge has improved, even though Rosalie still gets vexed if she feels Miss Grey is not giving her all her attention. Apart from minor changes, she still appears to be the vain, selfish creature she ever was and cannot imagine how Miss Grey can prefer to go away to her home on holiday rather than stay behind to see her in her 'splendid new dress' and the ball-room decked out in readiness! Miss Grey remains adamant, as she always does once her decision is taken. She even uses strong vocabulary to convince Rosalie 'I cannot bear the thoughts of a Christmas spent from home; and moreover my sister is going to be married' (p.119). The ensuing dialogue on her sister's fiancé, Mr. Richardson, the Vicar of the neighbouring parish, whom Agnes, in answer to Rosalie's questions, describes as 'comfortable', 'decent' and 'middling' of age, living in 'a quiet little vicarage, with an ivy-clad porch, an old-fashioned garden', (p.120) renders Rosalie quite distracted as she struggles to imagine how Miss Grey's sister will bear the boredom of such a fate. After all Agnes's words of wisdom, Rosalie still cannot imagine such a life spent with someone Miss Grey points out as 'good, wise' and 'amiable'. The mere mention of Agnes's sister having to look after her husband's poor parishioners 'in accordance with our mother's example' (p.121) (which Agnes adds in her customary way of never missing an opportunity to indicate to her pupils how such a life is indeed a worthy one), goes just too far for poor Rosalie to be able to countenance such a fate. Consequently, her attitude to marriage emerges here, contrasting sharply with Mary Grey's example, and we learn that, even though she dislikes Sir Thomas Ashby and calls him 'the wickedest' man she knows, she *will* marry him just to get the title of Lady Ashby and live in Ashby Park. Her fear of being an old maid makes her opt for this opportunity even if she dislikes him: 'if I could be always young, I would be always single' and then 'I would coquet with all the world' until her age dictated that she should marry 'some high-born, rich, indulgent husband whom, on the other hand, fifty ladies were dying to have' (p.128). Herein lies her true ambition to be ever beautiful, flirtatious and better than other young ladies. Agnes's dry response, 'Well, as long as you entertain those views, keep single by all means, and never marry at all: not even to escape the infamy of old maidenhood', is lost on Rosalie, unable to comprehend such irony, which is spoken, nevertheless, with not just a touch of disappointed desperation on Agnes's part.

Miss Grey's impressions are also sought by Rosalie on the new curate. Agnes declares him to be not particularly ugly and with a good style of reading the lessons, 'praying earnestly and sincerely from his own heart' (p.130). This description of hers and her thoughts on Mr. Weston's good preaching of the Gospel contrasts widely with her mental picture of Mr. Hatfield's undignified haste to place the Squire's wife and daughters into their carriage whilst not deigning to notice the governess (as happens frequently with all the gentry who frequent the church and visit Horton Lodge). She emphasises the difference between the two clergymen and, although humorously put, manages also to conjure up the sadness and loneliness of a governess's position and the hypocrisy of some of the clergy and churchgoers, like Rosalie, who, in pursuit of male attention from Harry Meltham, attends church twice on Sundays. One of Matilda's unfailingly direct remarks to Rosalie on the way home from church, 'I'm not always grubbing after money like you and mamma' (p.136), shows how she is quite aware of what her elder sister is doing in accepting marriage with a man she does not love. Miss Grey has at least succeeded in getting across her point of view on this particular issue to the younger of her charges. Rosalie, as always, pretends to be shocked and reproves Miss Grey for allowing Matilda to speak in this way. Agnes's clever response to her, which emphasises that in her capacity as governess there is no way she could stop it, 'I can't possibly prevent it, Miss Murray', shows her ability to easily comprehend Rosalie's little games and double standards. This double attendance at church permits Agnes to hear and praise inwardly 'the evangelical truth' of Mr. Weston's doctrine as opposed to Mr. Hatfield's dry approach and homing in on Church discipline, 'rites and ceremonies, apostolic succession, the duty of reverence and obedience to the clergy, the atrocious criminality of Dissent, the absolute necessity of observing all the forms of godliness . . . the necessity of deferential obedience from the poor to the rich' (p.133). Here Anne voices her distaste of those Calvinists by whom God was viewed as 'a terrible task-master, rather than a benevolent father' (p.133). This comparison is treated in a much more entertaining way than we see in Hannah More's authorial interventions, in her one and only novel, *Coelebs in search of a Wife*, where she talks along similar lines to Anne but forces her Evangelism upon her readers instead of, like Anne Brontë, allowing them to absorb it through her humour.

Agnes is occasionally asked to accompany the young ladies to see the poor cottagers on their father's estate. She prefers to go alone as she sincerely enjoys meeting them but, when accompanied by Rosalie and Matilda, finds it difficult to reconcile the behaviour of the young ladies towards the poor folk. Once again, she blames 'their defective education' for their lack of consideration, knowing that she has taught them for only two years, and was introduced to them when Rosalie was more or less formed both educationally and spiritually. This is yet another veiled appeal to all parents on Anne's behalf, warning them to discipline and guide their children more clearly and to watch carefully over those engaged to teach them. This is based on Anne's knowledge of Proverbs 19 v.18: 'Discipline your son, for in that there is hope; do not be a willing party to his death'. Agnes grieves at the young girls' arrogance towards the cottagers, whom they consider as 'stupid and brutish' and therefore lucky to receive gifts of money or clothing from them. In return, they expect the reward of being adored as 'angels of light condescending to minister to their necessities, and enlighten their humble dwellings' (p.139). Agnes is merely voicing Anne's own disgust at what she herself witnessed in her posts as governess, most probably with the Robinsons, for her aunt or father could never be supposed to have held such an attitude to the poor. Agnes forms a friendship with one of the poor cottagers, Nancy Brown, who has severe inflammation of the eyes, and goes to see her whenever she can, in order to read to her. It is at Nancy's home that she hears praise of Mr. Weston, whose visits give Nancy much more comfort and genuine pleasure than do Mr. Hatfield's, for the latter troubles her greatly with his constant remarks that: 'He that is born of God cannot commit sin'. Anne herself had suffered greatly from such Calvinist principles at Roe Head School, and reveals, through Mr. Hatfield, the pretentious, proud preacher of doom, the damaging effect that statements such as anyone who sins is condemned to Hell and Damnation can have on a person's life. Nancy is rendered distraught by Hatfield's uncomforting words and is offered no help by him in subsequent church visits even to the point of overhearing him describe her to the new curate, Mr. Weston, as 'a canting old fool' (p.147). Anne leads us to understand that it is immediately after this statement that Mr. Weston begins his regular visits to Nancy to help her to understand that the Gospel is one of love not of condemnation, thereby drawing our attention to the good nature and solid Christian principles of this new curate. Again we are presented with the two contrasting figures of Mr. Hatfield, who kicks Nancy's cat across the room, and of Mr. Weston, who, knowing Nancy loves the cat, strokes and smiles at her. Indeed, Mr. Weston's kindness enables Nancy to understand many verses in the Bible which have been worrying her intensely in the light of the question of eternal punishment, and helps her realise how to assist others. On her visits to other poor labourers, Agnes hears more praise of Mr. Weston, which gives her something good to reflect upon in her lonely drudgery. She misses so much having someone around 'whose conversation was calculated to render [her] better' (p.155). This is another reminder that the effect of proximity to people whose behaviour is 'fatiguing folly' is 'a serious evil, both in its immediate effects and the consequences that were likely to ensue' (p.155). The theory of the rotten apple affecting those around it is used more intensely in *The Tenant*, where Helen voices Anne's very real fear that her intellect would deteriorate, her heart petrify, her soul contract and particularly that her very 'moral perceptions should become deadened' and 'her distinctions of right and wrong confounded', and all her 'better faculties be sunk at last' (p.156) through her nearness to her evil husband. Anne had in her time seen much that was bad and had witnessed the irreparable damage to her own brother, corrupted by consorting with evil people; hence her very real worries for those placed in such proximity.

Miss Murray's double visits to church continue, not from her love of God but rather from her love of human admiration and flattery. The lowliness of the position of a governess is further highlighted by Anne, who describes how, on one of these walks back from church, Agnes is subjected to very rude treatment from the young ladies and gentleman whose gaze passes over her head as if she were simply not there. On some occasions she lingers behind them, annoying herself by making it look as if she acknowledges her inferiority, which she does not. One afternoon Mr. Weston surprises her by catching up with her and picking three primroses, which she is in the act of admiring. He hands them to her and, after conversing with her about their parents and how his were now deceased, proceeds to claim that 'the best of happiness is . . . the power and the will to be useful' (p.172). His sentiments match her own so perfectly and the reader can see, in advance, that Agnes will dream of this meeting and preserve the flowers he has given her. Anne makes one of her rare interventions at this point to state that she 'began this book with the intention of conceding nothing; that those who liked might have the benefit of perusing a fellow-creature's heart; but' – and here she stresses the word 'some' – 'we have some thoughts that all angels in heaven are welcome to behold, but not our brother-men – not even the best and kindest amongst them.' (pp.173/4). This statement resembles her opening words to this novel, where she states that she will 'candidly lay before the public what I could not disclose to the most intimate friend' (p.15). Her initial statement, however, has been amended and given certain reservations. This clever stylistic device of repetition with a hint of change serves to emphasise the personal issue at stake, that however much one wishes to warn and help others by openly feeding them with valuable advice, a point is always reached where certain thoughts cannot be divulged but only shared with one's Maker.

Ridiculed by Rosalie, Agnes calls the girls' teasing about Mr. Weston 'humbug' but naïvely reveals she has met him previously in Nancy's cottage. That night Agnes's prayers reflect her agitation as she struggles to decide whether her motives are simply for another's welfare, that other being Mr. Weston, or is she in love! She presses the petals of one of the primroses between the leaves of her Bible to 'keep them always'. This Romantic touch, a gesture worthy of Walter Scott, is not totally out of keeping with the pragmatic Miss Grey, for the essentially good and honest approach of Mr. Weston has not failed to please even her greatly. Her behaviour, however, although Romantic in private, is in public what could be commended by all good conduct books, for she keeps silent on her secret thoughts about Edward Weston, sharing them only with God. This is in total contrast with the behaviour of Rosalie, who actively seeks out male admiration and even uses deceit to obtain it, such as when she claims to Agnes that she has gone out to read a new novel, insisting that Miss Grey stay behind to finish off one of her watercolours. In actual effect, she has no intention of reading and deliberately sits in a field to be 'discovered' by Mr. Hatfield, and thereby inveigle him into proposing marriage to her, so that she can boast of the conquest of his heart. The reproof Miss Grey receives from Mrs. Murray, who happens to get to know of this: 'if you – if any governess had but half a mother's watchfulness and half a mother's anxious care I should be saved this trouble' (p.180), cuts Agnes to the quick, for she knows the truth of the situation. Consequently we, the readers, also aware of the mother's deceitful ways, note her expression of great anxiety and care with some suspicion, knowing that this is yet another outward display of emotions for effect on her part, for, inwardly, she is only interested in not allowing her daughter to spoil her chances of gaining Sir Thomas Ashby in marriage. This deceit we see reproduced unfortunately in Rosalie herself, proving that 'Parents are' indeed 'patterns'. Indeed, Rosalie's remark, 'when we go out, mamma won't let me flirt with anybody but Sir Thomas' although it seems to be common knowledge that he is 'the greatest scamp in Christendom' (pp.183/4) emphasizes the fact that Rosalie's mother knows far more against him than her daughter, but has still conditioned her daughter to marry him: 'he'll be all right when he's married, as mamma says; and reformed rakes make the best husbands, everybody knows'. (p.184) Rosalie has been kept ignorant, as was the custom of the day, so that she would not question her 'duty' to marry well, and 'well' has to be, solely for material gain, not for love nor mutual respect. Rosalie, guided in this way, states 'I must have Ashby Park, whoever shares it with me' (p.184). Agnes knows her words of advice are not being heeded by Rosalie, and a second example of Rosalie's deceitfulness occurs again in the field, where, this time, both she and Miss Murray are sitting. Agnes, unaware of the advancing Mr. Hatfield, is sent off hurriedly by Miss Murray with a half-a-crown gift for a consumptive labourer, only to catch a glimpse of the approaching Mr. Hatfield when she is some distance away. In any case, the gift is much needed and also allows Agnes to meet Mr. Weston who is also en route to Mark Wood's humble abode. Mr. Weston shows interest in what she is reading and in the little terrier, called Snap, at her feet, whom she explains is really Matilda's pup, which has come to follow herself for affection. Mr. Weston quietly converses with Agnes until they separate and she meets up with Miss Murray. On her way back, Rosalie's deceit becomes even more apparent as she claims to Agnes that Mr. Hatfield had come upon her by accident. She brushes this issue aside, however, in her excitement and haste to divulge the important news of his proposal and of her refusal. She glibly tells Agnes of even more lies she has used in order to reply to Mr. Hatfield's question as to whether she would have married him if he had been wealthy like Sir Hugh Meltham, admitting to Agnes that her response had been indeed 'a great lie' but 'that he could not imagine I was saying anything more than the actual truth.' (p.190). Even the promise she has made to Hatfield, not to divulge his proposal to anyone else, is broken instantly by her telling Agnes and fully intending to tell her news to her sister and to Brown, who 'will blazon it, or be the means of blazoning it, throughout the country' (p.194). Agnes is horrified at Rosalie's perfidy and at her unfounded delight at being able to show her mother that she had no cause to worry about her. She is so proud at what she has achieved and especially at Hatfield's 'agony of mind' that Agnes feels compelled to reprove her charge sharply. Miss Murray, however, simply views her scolding as a want of sympathy and even as possible envy on her part, failing to realize how her heartless vanity has truly disgusted her governess. Agnes wonders 'why so much beauty should be given to those who made so bad a use of it, and denied to some who would make it a benefit to both themselves and others', but concludes that 'God knows best' (p.196). Here again, Anne is giving us a lesson that she might well have picked up from her reading of the Scriptures, and also from her reading of Mary Brunton's *Discipline*, where reliance on God rather than on man's ability or appearance is uppermost. We see how Rosalie, having received instruction from Agnes very late in her formation, has changed very little, for her knowledge is still scanty and her attitude tainted by the education she has received at the hands of her mother, and of the other educators, chosen without due care and attention to her spiritual welfare.

At this stage, Rosalie's whole world revolves around herself and bored, she begins to look for new conquests to distract her and decides to turn her attention onto Mr. Weston, whom she has seen paying some attention to Agnes. Indeed, she knew that he had even shown some interest in Agnes's 'moral and intellectual capacities' (p.204). Rosalie determines to 'fix that man' (p.206), and make him dream of her, whilst poor Agnes is compelled to fulfil her duty and carry on as if all is well, although she is intensely worried at the state of her heart being 'more bent upon the creature than the creator' (p.208). Rosalie continues to make a play for Mr. Weston's attentions at church and elsewhere, telling Agnes that she means to accept Sir Thomas on the following Tuesday, but, for something to do, will meantime take up Mr. Weston. To further her ends with Mr. Weston, Rosalie refuses to allow Agnes to visit a poor old lady at the Porter's Lodge, instead visiting her herself so that she can be seen by Mr. Weston to be the truly charitable one. Nor will Rosalie allow Agnes to make further visits to Nancy, for fear she might meet up with her new target man and she gives Agnes, rather spitefully on one occasion, a piece of music to copy out and keep her occupied until bed-time. Agnes realises 'the whole contrivance' (p.213), but can do nothing to prevent Rosalie's tricks. However, she does begin to pay more attention to her appearance but feels no pride in her 'pale hollow cheek, and ordinary brown hair'. At least, however, she notes modestly that there is some intellect 'in the forehead . . . expression in the dark grey eyes' (p.214), but that is all. At her lowest point, we see her recognize how foolish it is to wish for beauty but the reader knows how much she would have welcomed this 'gift of God' (p.216). This scene, written before Charlotte Brontë wrote *Jane Eyre*, resembles Jane's desire for beauty, which she expresses forcibly to Mr. Rochester when she tells him that, if she had been beautiful, things would have turned out differently. Many nineteenth-century writers echoed this longing for beauty, as can be seen in *Le Journal d'Eugénie de Guérin*, a letter diary, written over a period of about eleven years, from 1834 to 1848, where Eugénie stresses her longing to have been born beautiful, for, if she had been, others would have loved her far more.[10]

Finally, Sir Thomas Ashby's proposal is accepted and, although pleased with her achievement, Rosalie wants to delay the ceremony. Agnes, sticking true to her principles and managing to show her charge no malice at what has been going on, once again tries to advise her, before it is too late, not to go through with the wedding. Miss Murray only mocks her advice, stating her only reason for delay is securing more time in which to wreak havoc amongst the young gentlemen of her acquaintance, before being incapacitated from further mischief of that kind by her marriage. After hearing this, even Agnes's kindness and patience is exhausted and she 'has no more pity for her' (p.218), realising that Rosalie deserves what she will get. The marriage is arranged for 1 June, but, meantime, Rosalie continues her deceitful actions, even receiving letters from young Harry Meltham and trying, without success, to re-animate Mr. Hatfield's sentiments for her. In addition to all this, she employs all her female charms to captivate Mr. Weston. She suddenly develops a taste to be 'extremely beneficent to the poor cottagers' (p.221) but apart from this more harmless hypocrisy, she also uses blatant lies to try to turn away for good Mr. Weston's interest in Agnes. She tells him that, although Agnes is quite well, she has no desire to attend church, when the truth of the matter is that she and Matilda had set off deliberately before Agnes even knew they had left! Mr. Weston continues to ask politely about Miss Grey, but is told a succession of lies to put him off. Agnes, informed by Matilda of Rosalie's malicious remarks, can only grieve inwardly at Rosalie's spitefulness. At this point, Agnes (for Anne) reiterates what she stated at the very beginning of the novel, that it is easier to share such matters with strangers than with close friends, saying, 'I fear, by this time, the reader is well nigh disgusted with the folly and weakness I have so freely laid before him. I never disclosed it then, and would not have done so had my own sister or my mother been with me in the house'.

'I was a close and resolute dissembler – in this one case at least. My prayers, my tears, my wishes, fears, and lamentations, were witnessed by myself and Heaven alone' (p.226). Anne's well-known passage on the relief poetry affords those who are 'harassed by sorrows or anxieties' follows on, emphasising what has been her own personal method of dealing with the suffering at the Parsonage, which she has been helpless to do anything about, over the last few years. Agnes, who has suffered greatly, at the hands of her spiteful pupils, voices Anne's agony, and shows how a lack of faith, of knowledge and of serious charitable occupation in a female can cause her to dwell entirely on her personal attractions to the detriment of her integrity. Indeed, this can even lead to the destruction of others, as actually happened in Branwell's case, corrupted as he was by Mrs. Robinson's seductive arts. Anne tells us, via Agnes, that she has resorted to this 'secret source of consolation' of using poetry, two or three times previously, when suffering from home-sickness. Indeed, this is apparent in many of her poems, which reveal such an intensity of sadness and loneliness as in her verses in *Agnes Grey*:

> 'Oh, they have robbed me of the hope
> My spirit held so dear;
> They will not let me hear that voice
> My soul delights to hear.
>
> They will not let me see that face
> I so delight to see;
> And they have taken all thy smiles,
> And all thy love from me.
>
> Well, let them seize on all they can; –
> One treasure still is mine, –
> A heart that loves to think on thee,
> And feels the worth of thine.' (p.227)

Although the above poem is usually attributed to Anne's love of William Weightman's voice and smiles, the 'they' in question is evidently meant here to be the Miss Murrays, who have even deprived her of the affection of Snap, by sending him away to be put down. Also, at this point in time, her father's health is worsening and the poem shows Anne's utter reliance on God and the Evangelistic thrust of her writings.

After Miss Murray's wedding, Agnes, unable to say a lie by offering her congratulations to her former pupil, wishes her instead 'true happiness and the best of blessings' as Rosalie rushes off on her honeymoon in Europe. At this, her pupil returns to embrace Agnes with far more affection than Agnes had thought possible of her and then leaves with tears in her eyes. Agnes truly forgives her for the injury she has done her, and, in maternal fashion, prays God to pardon her too. That evening, Agnes manages, at last, to visit Nancy Brown to apologize for her long absence, but, and here we see her feelings on her sleeve in her statement, 'no one came', and, indeed, she has to wait quite a while before Mr. Weston re-appears in her life.

Matilda's mother, exultant at having successfully disposed of one daughter now turns her attention to the other, finding her sadly lacking in manners and the necessary graces to attract a husband. Aroused by this fact, she begins to exert her authority and forbids Matilda the yards, stables, kennels and coach-house in an attempt to get her transformed into a fashionable young lady. Many arguments ensue between mother and daughter for the relationship between them is based on such trivial matters, and certainly not on solid Christian principles. Naturally, Agnes is blamed for Matilda's deficiencies by Mrs. Murray's 'implied reproaches' and 'veiled insults' (p.234), being told by her rather cruelly to exert herself a little more and to acquire some 'delicate tact', which would give her 'a proper influence' (p.236) over Matilda's mind. Agnes is never allowed by Mrs. Murray to defend herself, for, as a paid employee, she is expected to listen but not to respond. From the beginning of her engagement, Mrs. Murray has treated Agnes coldly, but gradually over time, she begins to lay aside her airs and graces, becoming as attached to her as it was possible for her to be to someone of Agnes's 'character and position: for she seldom lost sight, for above half an hour at a time, of the fact of my being a hireling and a poor curate's daughter'. The irony is cutting and the contrast between Mrs. Murray's initial and later response to Agnes all the more impressive, in that the reader sees Mrs. Murray learning to respect her governess's 'good principles, the truth she spoke and her endeavours to make inclination bow to duty' (p.104). Unfortunately, it was too late for Agnes to change her employer's attitude on arranged marriages.

Matilda, now watched over so carefully by her mother, is compelled to find other means of occupying herself than her previous recreational pursuits, so consents, out of boredom, to accompany Agnes on her visits to the cottagers, thereby unwittingly helping Agnes to meet up with Mr. Weston. At last, the meeting takes place and Agnes is able to answer truthfully for herself to his enquiries as to whether it was Rosalie's mother's wish that Rosalie marry Sir Thomas Ashby. Agnes replies that it was, but that it was also Miss Murray's 'for she always laughed at my attempts to dissuade her from the step' (p.238). Mr. Weston is pleased by the honesty of her response and Agnes, or even more her creator, replies to his remark that Mrs. Murray will have difficulty justifying her conduct by telling him that, 'It seems unnatural, but some people think rank and wealth the chief good, and if they can secure that for their children, they think they have done their duty'. Anne then uses her fictional hero to air another truth on the subject, which is that it is very strange that parents who have been married themselves should judge things so falsely. An instance of this falseness is then put before his very gaze in the example of Matilda's admitting to him that she had pretended to want to save a hare, but, in reality, was delighted that it was killed by her dog, Prince, in, what she terms, 'a noble chase'. The example seems deliberately positioned here to convince Mr. Weston, and Anne's readers too, of the deceit practised by the whole Murray family, which has been inherited from the false judgment of the parents and passed down to the children. Later, Mr. Weston returns to offer Agnes some bluebells, at which point in time she has a chance to remedy the remarks that Rosalie had made about her preferring books to attending church or visiting the cottagers.

Less than two days later, she receives a letter from her home telling her that her father's life is in danger, but is only permitted by Mrs. Murray to leave for the Parsonage at a date which was too late to allow her to see her father alive. Plans are subsequently made at her home for her and her mother to start up their own school and for Agnes to leave her post at the Murrays.

Agnes's mother's integrity is further placed in evidence when she refuses her father's overtures to reinstate her in his family, if she will just repent of her 'unfortunate marriage'. He tempts her with the thought that her daughters would then have a legacy at his death. Mrs. Grey's decision to uphold her marriage and to refuse her father's offer meets with the full approval of her daughters, in whom she has evidently instilled her own good virtues. Anne offers advice here for all those grieving at having lost loved ones, suggesting that the poor who have no leisure to mourn their dead are in a better position for 'is not active employment the best remedy for overwhelming sorrow – the surest antidote for despair?' (p.249). This well-meant advice is evidently of importance to Anne herself, who had had to cope away from home when both William Weightman and her Aunt had died. Also, in her situation in the Parsonage she must have been ever-conscious of the precariousness of Branwell's life and have kept herself active to avoid too much time to think about it. Indeed, it is applicable too to all unmarried women, who have to earn a living, encouraging them to work hard and to rely on God in order to get through such sad times.

Agnes manages to tell Mr. Weston that she will be leaving her post in a month's time and he tactfully asks about her mother, exhibiting tender parental feelings and great delicacy in his approach to her. Over three years have elapsed since Agnes joined the Murray household and she, now nearly twenty-three years of age, is reassured to find that her years of instructing Matilda have evidently borne some fruit, for, at least, Matilda has managed to conquer her deceitfulness. In her last week of service, Mr. Weston once again draws near to Agnes to ask her whether it would be of any consequence whether they meet again. Dear Agnes, ever truthful and plain-speaking, can only answer in the affirmative!

Her return home is glanced over rather rapidly and we learn of the new school, based at A–, which recalls the school that the young Brontë sisters had dreamt of having. The idea of a school of their own is commented on by Emily Brontë in her diary paper of 30 July 1841, where she mentions the scheme. Also, in Anne's diary paper of the same date, it is mentioned as not yet being a definite plan, although Anne disliked her situation at that time as governess to the Robinsons and wished to change it for another. Aunt Branwell even offers them a loan for the purpose, but Charlotte and Emily determine to spend some time in Brussels to improve their qualifications and to gain French and 'a dash of German' before setting up the school, and eventually the whole thing fails. The idea of starting their own school might well have originated from Aunt Branwell's reminiscing to them about a school that she and her sisters, Charlotte and Maria, had in Chapel Street, Penzance, for their school had been situated in a similar seaside resort to that Brontë uses for Agnes's mother's school based at A–. Aunt Branwell might well have told her young nieces of the school-room built behind her home. According to an article by Ivy Holgate about the Branwells at Penzance, the fact of there having been a school is supported by a letter by Mr. Breffit stating 'there was an old school-room behind 25 Chapel Street built by one of the Branwells and perhaps the daughters carried on a school there too'.[11]

While working at her mother's school, Agnes is invited to stay with Lady Ashby, her former pupil, as a friend rather than as a former governess, for Rosalie is desirous of engaging Agnes as governess for her baby girl. Evidently, Agnes's attempts at reforming her character have caused Rosalie to reflect on what could have happened if she had followed Agnes's advice and to wish for better things for her child. She tells Agnes, 'you shall bring it up in the way it should go, and make a better woman of it than its mamma' (p.265). Agnes accepts her invitation to stay but not her invitation to tutor her child. Once arrived, she hopes against hope that she will meet up with Mr. Weston, only to find that he had left the area a month previously. Rosalie welcomes her with great kindness and 'with unaffected pleasure' and Agnes is truly delighted to find that Matilda too has greatly improved. John and Charles, however, have turned out, as she feared, to be 'fine, bold, unruly, mischievous boys' (p.272). In other words, they had become what was expected of them by Victorian society, considering the lack of authority and discipline exerted over them by their parents and their school. The contrast is quite marked between Rosalie's and Matilda's three years' tuition at Agnes's hands, an education carried out with kindness, strictness and adherence to the will of God, with that of John and Charles, who had never been subjected to discipline, nor had any adherence to a code of values. Because of such a training, Rosalie, unfortunately too late to benefit herself, has become aware of how things could have turned out differently if she had but listened to the advice offered her by her governess and is hopeful that such a fate as she is enduring can be avoided for her child.

Anne, via Agnes, suggests ways of helping Rosalie cope with the difficulties she is experiencing with her husband and her mother-in-law. Agnes learns that most of the time her husband has nothing to do but 'to sot over his wine' (p.278), and advises Rosalie to spend more time with him and to try her best to help him to give up such habits. Rosalie, however, cannot accept this as part of her brief, for, never having tried to please anyone other than herself, she cannot bring herself to please her husband, someone whom she feels should be pleasing her instead. Consequently, when Agnes arrives, no partnership nor relationship exists between Rosalie and Sir Thomas, and Rosalie confesses to her former governess how terribly unhappy she is and how much she wishes she had heeded Agnes's warnings. As she says, 'it is too late to regret that now. And besides, mamma ought to have known better than either of us, and she never said anything against it – quite the contrary' (p.281). Her words reflect the true state of affairs not only between Mrs. Murray and Rosalie but also between many young daughters and their mothers in Anne's age, and reveal how Mrs. Murray, herself a victim of Victorian culture and mis-information, had not thought fit to warn her daughter against marrying such a man. Rosalie has been left to discover to her cost that her husband is a gambler, a womaniser and a drunk and she longs to be single once again. Agnes can only encourage her by exhorting her 'to seek consolation in doing her duty to God and man, to put her trust in Heaven, and solace herself with the care and nurture of her little daughter, assuring her she would be amply rewarded by witnessing its progress in strength and wisdom, and receiving its genuine affection'. Again, we see Anne's emphasis on the importance of relationships – a relationship between God and man, between a wife and her husband, and between a mother and her child. Agnes urges Rosalie, voicing Anne's advice to any wife whose husband brings her nothing but sorrow, to try and change the situation 'first, by gentle reasoning, by kindness, example, and persuasion to try and ameliorate her husband, and then when she had done all she could, if she still find him incorrigible, to endeavour to abstract herself from him – to wrap herself up in her own integrity and trouble herself as little about him as possible' (p.282). Anne is certainly not invoking women's legal rights here, as does Wollstonecraft, but instead shows that she is far more concerned with trying to obtain a Christian, rather than a political, solution to the problem. In fact, in *The Tenant,* we see Helen living out this very way of life, after having done her utmost to change her husband. Agnes tells Rosalie that 'the best way to enjoy yourself is to do what is right and to hate nobody' and advises her, although not much older than her former pupil, in a motherly way, to befriend her mother-in-law. Anne's lessons to any married lady living in unhappiness are clear and practical, for she advises her to do her duty, trusting in God at all times and to enjoy the parenting of her child. Agnes, then, with heavy heart, goes back home to her mother's school.

Once there, she feels the need, early one morning, to escape to the sands, as one can visualise Anne having done in Scarborough before her daily duties with the Robinsons began. Refreshed and invigorated by the sea-air, she catches a glimpse of a gentleman behind her, 'a little dark speck of a dog running before him' (p.287). As in all happy endings, he turns out to be none other than the hero, Mr. Weston, with her very own dog, Snap, rescued and cared for by him. To Agnes, the meeting seems ordained by Providence, 'considering all the circumstances of the case' (p.289). Mr. Weston's lack of visits to her is explained away by his inability to trace her home and a meeting is arranged for him to call on her mother the following day. He is now, he tells her, the Vicar of F–, a village about two miles distant from A–, and receives a £300 annual stipend and a respectable Vicarage. The ingredients are in place for a Romantic conclusion,[12] especially as he remarks that 'I have nothing but solitude to complain of, and nothing but a companion to wish for'. The visit and ensuing visits take place, with Agnes's mother initially replying that she had never heard Agnes mention him before. In view of Agnes's mother's discretion and Agnes's, as well as Anne's, desire for privacy, this remark does not surprise the reader over-much. Eventually, after a cautious courtship, the marriage proposal is given and accepted, having been cleared in advance by Agnes's mother.

At this late point in the novel, we are told that all this has been taken from Agnes's diary and that she has become the wife of Edward Weston. There is great emphasis placed on the relationship between them as, we are also told, their trials will be borne together and they will endeavour to fortify themselves 'against the final separation'. The novel ends, in revealing Agnes's great love for her husband, with the statement that she defies anybody to blame Edward Weston 'as a pastor, a husband, or a father'. Anne now shows Agnes, whose parenting experience in her posts as governess stands her in good stead, as a caring mother preparing to educate her three children, Edward, Agnes and little Mary, and assuring us that 'they shall want no good thing that a mother's care can give' (p.301). Even the choice of names indicates a re-run of Agnes's and Edward's own infancy, as evidently both sets of parents have succeeded in bringing up their children in a similar way to respect the same values and to trust in God.

In this novel, Anne distinguishes between the first and second posts held by Agnes, in that her time with the Bloomfields is seen to exhaust her, proving to be over-strenuous physically, even for a very young woman. The unruly children she teaches only begin to make slight progress at the point of her dismissal, even after the maximum efforts she has expended. Her time with the Murrays affects her more in a spiritual way for she becomes dispirited by her seemingly unsuccessful attempts to morally reform and humanize the two girls. At length, however, showing Anne's emphasis on the need for perseverance in such tasks, her diligence pays off, as is evident not only from Agnes's visit to Lady Ashby's but also in the many illustrations Anne gives, which reveal the effects of Agnes's imaginative and flexible programme of education. We see her constantly making adjustments to the limitations imposed upon her by her employers. Through this, Anne emphasises the exemplary way in which Agnes lives out what she expects her charges to do and how she uses her steadfastness and humour (evidently contributing factors to her success), to gain the love and respect of Rosalie and Matilda and even of Mrs. Murray herself.

Anne intervenes very little in her tale, basing much on the reader's intelligence to understand from the double-angled scenes she presents, what is the best method of proceeding to help young beings to change their attitudes and to be better equipped to cope with the trials of their times. Anne's presence in *Agnes Grey* appears far lighter and she seems less embroiled in the plot, as she writes of Agnes's experiences in what George Moore described as the 'most perfect piece of narrative prose'. At the time of writing, although she was about half-way through the three years of misery caused by Branwell at the Parsonage, her humour is very much present and contrasts starkly with the darker scenes of *The Tenant* yet to come. Aware of the need to point out the indolence of wealthy ladies, such as her former employers, and the decadent attitude of the gentry towards education and the oppression of women, Anne shows great courage as she reveals in *Agnes Grey* what life was really like behind the closed doors of the outwardly respectable Victorian homes. As Stevie Davies puts it, 'she has analysed her culture fearlessly'.[13]

In *Agnes Grey,* a governess narrates how she parents other people's children, whereas in *The Tenant of Wildfell Hall,* although the main parenting is carried out by Helen, we see examples of child rearing by multiple characters, mothers, fathers, aunts and uncles, as varied as the narrators themselves. Indeed, in *Agnes Grey*, Agnes, before becoming a parent herself, brings up other people's children and learns from the mistakes committed by the parents themselves. However, in *The Tenant*, we meet with a more detailed follow-up of such mistakes, and we see, the results of Helen's uncontrolled and emotional acceptance of the wrong sort of man for a husband, and the hideous effect which bad parenting has had on Arthur Huntingdon, Annabella Wilmot, Walter Hargrave and Lord Lowborough. Indeed, there is only one truly happy marriage in Anne's first novel, and that is Agnes's own union with Edward Weston, for even her parents' marriage is imperfect in that her father is directed away from his better understanding towards the pursuit of more money, leading eventually to his financial ruin. We also see the excellent results of good parenting in Agnes herself, her sister, Mary, and indeed in Edward Weston, whom, we are informed by Anne, will pass on such skills to their own children. In *The Tenant*, Helen's upbringing by her devout, well-informed and caring aunt trains her to be an excellent parent, whose integrity is contrasted briefly with that of Anne's second governess, Miss Myers, (who is presented in a totally unfavourable light, compared with Anne's first governess, Agnes Grey).

2. Portrait of a girl with a dog, c.1840-1845, drawn by Anne Brontë. The dog looks very much like Flossy, the King Charles spaniel which the Robinsons gave to Anne in 1843. This drawing could well represent the dog passed on to Agnes by the Murray girls in Agnes Grey. By permission of the Brontë Society Parsonage Museum.

3. Portrait of a child's head, drawn in pencil by Anne Brontë and dated 15 November 1837. This is one of a series copied from prints by Anne whilst at Roe Head School.

Reproduced by permission of the Brontë Society Museum.

4. Portrait of a child's head, looking upwards, drawn in pencil on thin card by Anne Brontë on 31 August 1837.

By permission of the Brontë Society Parsonage Museum.

4. A copy of a print of A. E. Gray's painting of St. Mary's Church, Castle Road, Scarborough, where Anne was buried on 30 May 1849.
Courtesy: St. Mary's Scarborough P.C.C.

Chapter Three:

The Tenant of Wildfell Hall

By the time Anne started writing *The Tenant of Wildfell Hall* in early 1847, Branwell, as has been already mentioned, was well and truly ensconced in his vicious habits. The years from July 1845 onwards had taken their toll on Anne's strength and spirits, and her second novel reveals quite a difference of approach to that of her first. *The Tenant* begins and ends with a letter written and narrated in the first person by Gilbert Markham on 10 June 1847, which might well have been the very date when Anne put pen to paper for this, her second novel. The letter refers back to the autumn of 1827, and embedded within its framework is 'the treasure' of 'a certain, faded old journal' which is an essential part of the 'full and faithful account' which Gilbert shares with his brother-in-law, Jack Halford, husband of his sister, Rose. After 'musing on past times' (p.34), Gilbert is 'in a very proper frame of mind for amusing' his correspondent or, in Anne's own voice, her public. This desire to both amuse and to be faithful to the essence of the account ties in with Anne's stated aim at the beginning of *Agnes Grey* and also in her *Preface to the Second Edition of The Tenant* (22 July 1848), where she declares her desire 'to tell the truth, for truth always conveys its own moral to those who are able to receive it'. Her intention is clear 'to reform the errors and abuses of society' and to contribute her 'humble quota' towards whispering a few such truths to her readers. Anne cannot limit her ambition in this novel to just giving 'innocent pleasure'. She states that amusement is all very well, but her true aim is to use her God-given talents, by all means to amuse, but also to benefit humanity: 'if I am able to amuse I will try to benefit too'. She is adamant that it is her duty to speak out, if necessary, 'an unpalatable truth', which shows she is certainly not writing just to become a popular best-selling author, for she is far more interested in her purpose and will not consent to conceal 'vice and vicious characters' (p.30), preferring to depict them as they really are. By being so honest she feels that she can help to impart to any 'rash youth' or 'thoughtless girl' a full knowledge of the facts of life in her times, so that they can be spared from living through the sin and misery of, as she says, being 'left to wring their bitter knowledge from experience'. Such an experience she goes on to describe in the life of her fictional heroine, Helen Graham/Huntingdon/Markham.

Although Charlotte realised that her sister 'must be honest . . . not varnish, soften or conceal' because 'she was a very sincere and practical Christian' (p.9), she was unable to approve of Anne's choice of subject. She found it distasteful and 'an entire mistake'[14]. Anne's choice of subject, however, reveals how, by this point in time, she had become more passionately embroiled, through life at the Parsonage, in Helen's sufferings. She had become more urgently concerned with educating the public so that, in their turn, they could eradicate such ills from society by educating correctly their offspring. She voices her fears through her fictional heroine, Helen, who, although well grounded in Christian values, is totally ignorant of life, innocent and inexperienced, as was acceptable to the society of her day. However, Helen was so physically attracted to her suitor that she is seen to be unable to control her emotions and to combat the sex appeal of this handsome but weak man. She sees only the outwardly captivating façade of Arthur Huntingdon, remaining unaware initially of the fact that inwardly he is degenerate. Helen's lack of knowledge of what indeed is sin causes her to act against her aunt's well-meaning warning of the dangers ahead of her, if she does marry this man. However, her wilful desire to have her own way also plays its part in her decision to marry Arthur, and her pride in her own ability to change him makes her disregard the many signs of his weakness, which are revealed to her personally not only by him, but also by her aunt, her servant, Rachel, and her friend, Milicent. Anne portrays her as a sincere Christian, very secure in her faith, but one who finds it impossible to accept that to reform Arthur's behaviour is outside her remit. This again is a feature of her age where women have foolishly begun to believe that they possess redemptive qualities and are able to change for the better everyone around them. The unfortunate life Helen leads after her marriage and the tormenting conduct to which she and her son are subjected constitute a large part of the contents of this novel. Throughout these tragic events, Anne uses her fictional heroine, to point out how things could well have been different if Arthur's parents had not always allowed him to do as he liked as a child. She intimates that all his mother and father have succeeded in doing is to spread the lie of their century: that by experiencing sin at first hand, a boy would be better able to resist indulging in it in the future. Anne feared a possible addiction to such sinful experiences, and emphasised the danger to the individual's eternal life if they remained unchecked either mentally or physically, once the passions have been unbridled. This nineteenth-century 'mal du siècle' is also captured by Alfred de Musset in his *Confessions d'un Enfant du Siècle,* where he reveals how much it was expected that a man experience all manner of forbidden fruits. This attitude of mind was very much evident in French writers of the period like Constant, Fromentin and Musset. Musset talks of experiencing sin and how, not just repetition of the same sins, but also the use of reflective analysis to anticipate them, can make them cease to be exciting, thereby creating unrest and boredom in a character. Anne's view is more concerned with the dangers of allowing such experiences at all.

Anne attributes blame to the education of girls, giving examples of how this can cause misery. Helen, although motherless and brought up by her aunt and uncle (like Anne herself, her father still lived), is forewarned by her aunt of the dangers of marrying an unsuitable man. Yet, up to the point of meeting Arthur Huntingdon, she is very innocent of society and, although offered her aunt's guidance, still remains not very knowledgeable of the consequences of yoking herself with a man already seeped in the evils of drink, drugs, gambling, and womanising. As the situation progresses, her aunt insists on giving her even stronger indications of Huntingdon's corrupt nature, but Helen seems incapable or wilfully determined not to understand their meaning and resolves to go ahead regardless.

Once wed, she very soon has to bear her husband's frequent trips away from home, missing him at first but gradually becoming relieved by his longer absences, caused by his sheer indulgence in debauched activities. However, out of Christian duty, she tenderly accepts her less than perfect husband on each of his returns, acting out the part of the 'angel in the house' as best she can. Indeed, she manages to bear everything he does, in saintly fashion, until the point at which Arthur turns his attention on their very young son and begins to involve him in his drinking sessions and bawdy evening parties. At this point, Helen prevaricates no longer, realising she must act before the damage inflicted on her precious child becomes so ingrained in him that he can no longer change his ways. Women living in the Victorian Age were unable to openly oppose their husbands, who had complete authority over them, so Helen has to train her son, in secret, to renounce the bad language his father teaches him and to hate the wine and strong liquors he is constantly tempting him to drink. She decides to offer him drinks of wine, or brandy and water, into which she introduces surreptitiously 'a small quantity of tartar-emetic – just enough to produce inevitable nausea and depression without positive sickness.' (p.375). In this way, as she says, she felt she was being instrumental in helping her son from falling into the snare of at least one evil. When her husband was at home, he was the master of his household with Helen entirely under his dominant control and therefore helpless to refuse to grant his insistent requests that his child be present at the gatherings of his lewd friends, which caused her intense heartache. Eventually, after much prayer and deliberation, she resolved on a daring plan to leave her husband and find refuge in her brother's and her own old and rather decrepit former family home: 'Wildfell Hall, a superannuated mansion of the Elizabethan era, built of dark grey stone, – venerable and picturesque to look at, but, doubtless, cold and gloomy enough to inhabit, with its thick stone mullions and little latticed panes, its time-eaten air-holes, and its too lonely, too unsheltered situation' (p.45). One wing had been adapted by her good brother to receive her there. Considering the times and the laws against women leaving their husbands, for whatever reason, it was natural that her brother had initially expressed a certain reluctance to help her. However, she managed, after a while, to convince him of the need to prepare their old home to receive her little party: 'where the broken windows and dilapidated roof had evidently been repaired, and where a thin wreath of smoke was curling up from the stack of chimneys' (p.46). Her brother himself had long since moved to a new and more commodious mansion. Unfortunately, Helen's initial plan to escape is discovered by Arthur, who immediately confiscates her household keys, money and also her painting materials, with which she intended to earn a living. Yet, although thwarted in this first attempt, she persists in her project, in which she is aided by a trusty servant who refuses secretly to carry out his master's orders to burn her easel and paints, so allowing Helen to retrieve them in readiness for her next and successful flight. Finally, she manages to leave the house, at dead of night, with her son, old nurse and very few possessions. This unusual act of daring, for Victorian times, is often quoted as proof of Anne's rather avant-garde, pro-feminist stance. However, there is not really any political slant intended by her, nor did she write such an episode simply to highlight the fact that women did not have any legal rights, a subject which was of great concern to Mary Wollstonecraft. She seemed to accept that that was the way things were and was more interested in making a stand from the Christian point of view. The act depicted by her was more to show that it was all that any caring mother could do under the circumstances. After all, she had tried everything that was reasonable to reform her husband and now had no alternative left to her other than to flee, in order to save her son from damnation. All the same, such a flight in the early nineteenth-century, even from such a husband, would indeed have been considered quite sensational and would have instantly lost the woman concerned her place in society. Divorce was out of the question and Anne's description of Helen adopting such drastic measures caused her to come in for some hefty, verbal abuse from contemporary critics, who labelled her both coarse and brutal for the relating of such a tale and the suggesting of such an outcome. Anne's fictional heroine speaks for her in defence of her husband whose descent into sin she points out as the fault of his upbringing rather than of his own disposition. Anne's totally flexible position on this issue of sinning is revealed here, showing her inner conviction that, even if one sins, one can be renewed and pardoned. This is depicted in Helen, who, although she has had a wonderful Christian upbringing by her loving aunt, still fails to make the right choice of marriage partner. However, Anne does not leave her in this state of failure, but portrays her, after enduring many trials, as achieving happiness with a good, principled man, thereby giving heart to her readers by reassuring them that it is never too late to act on the guide-lines she is proposing. An even more dramatic example of a girl losing her character by leaving her suitor and eloping with a rake occurs in *David Copperfield,* where Dickens portrays Little Emily, against her better judgement deserting Ham, and being led astray by David's friend, Steerforth, although her Uncle Peggotty had devoted his life to bringing her up in true Christian fashion. Emily, who is unmarried, is rescued by her uncle and able to begin a new life in Australia. Dickens, however, adopts a harsher approach than does Anne, who gives her heroine a second chance, for Ham dies shortly after Emily is discovered and she never finds happiness in marriage.

Helen, having escaped successfully from Grassdale, remains conscious of her duty as a wife, and, on receiving news of her husband's illness, returns home, after thirteen months of absence, to nurse him back to health, ever hopeful, at the same time, of getting him to repent. This is yet another example of Anne advocating the following of God's commandment to love others more than oneself, for Helen's return is not, as Arthur supposes, in order to avenge the wrongs he has committed to her, but more out of genuine commitment to her marriage vows of being united 'for better or for worse' and out of Christian duty. Helen is fully aware that, if Arthur recovers as a result of her care and attention, her own life and that of her beloved child will be menaced afresh by his behaviour; yet, she still returns. Her husband finds her motives for return entirely incomprehensible, especially when he learns that she has come home to 'benefit [him] as well to better [his] mind, as to alleviate [his] present sufferings' (pp.433-4). However, Helen's attempts to help her husband to master his passions, especially drink, prove unsuccessful, and she fails miserably to get him to adopt a healthier life-style. To the end of his life, sadly Arthur remains unable to curb his excesses but, at least, to her great comfort, in the last days, he does not constantly scorn the truth of there being a Heaven and Hell. Helen still fails, however, in her attempts to convince him of his need to repent and although Arthur is intensely fearful of death, he cannot bring himself to trust or comprehend such 'blessed truths' (p.451). When he realizes that he might not recover, he asks what Helen will do for him from Heaven if he is 'howling in hell-fire' and, at this point, Anne allows Helen, in answering his question, to voice her theory of Universal Salvation, that, even if one dies in ones sins, a purification process takes place which cleanses that person sufficiently for him to be able to enter Purgatory and eventually Heaven:

> 'If so, it will be because of the great gulf over which I cannot pass and if I could look complacently on in such a case, it would be only from the assurance that you were being purified from your sins, and fitted to enjoy the happiness I felt. But are you determined, Arthur, that I shall not meet you in heaven?' (p.446)

Arthur, terrified, clings to Helen before he dies. Her words, after his death, emphasise the importance to Anne of this doctrine and reflect the feelings she was to experience herself during those last painful days of Branwell's life:

> 'How could I endure to think that that poor trembling soul was hurried away to everlasting torment? It would drive me mad! But thank God I have hope – not only from a vague dependence on the possibility that penitence and pardon might have reached him at the last, but from the blessed confidence that, through whatever purging fires the erring spirit may be doomed to pass – whatever fate awaits it, still, it is not lost and God, who hateth nothing that He hath made, will bless it in the end!' (p.452).

This whole theme of religion, aimed here at the reform of an individual, is linked, as in *Agnes Grey,* with the themes of virtue and instruction. In Anne's first novel, we have seen how, in her first appointment, Agnes teaches young children to lead a virtuous life, and then, in her second post, older girls up to marriageable age, like Rosalie Murray. As Rosalie's governess, Agnes evidently finds it difficult to counteract the corrupt effects upon the two sisters caused by their parents' faulty education and total deficiency of basic Christian values. In *The Tenant of Wildfell Hall,* however, we are no longer confronted by a vain and empty-headed Rosalie agreeing to a marriage of convenience because her mind and heart are firmly impregnated by her mother's ideas of gaining wealth and status, but rather we see a young Helen Graham who, although carefully nurtured in true Christian fashion by her aunt (rather than by her drunken father), still manages to make a very bad choice. Rosalie too had thought it possible to change Sir Thomas Ashby, but for different reasons. She felt he adored her so much that he would 'let [her] have her own way'. Sadly, it does not take long for both girls to realise that their respective husbands are irreparably corrupt.

Anne gives us an example, of what can happen if guidance on such matters is given from a young age to someone of sufficient spirit to be able to carry through such ideas. Helen, who has learnt the hard way from her mistakes, is depicted as trying to teach the young Esther Hargrave, sister of one of her husband's motley band of friends, how to resist the influence of her mother, who is intent on marrying her off to a rich but corrupt suitor. Esther, in whom Helen has taken an interest since infancy, is a neighbour of hers and sister of Walter Hargrave, whom Helen instinctively dislikes. Mrs. Hargrave, over-proud of her son, is prepared to stint for herself and for her girls and even to marry them off to whomsoever is rich enough to ask for them. She is more interested in promoting her son's position in society by whatever means necessary so that her dear Walter can hold his head up high and spend lavishly on any indulgence he might need and 'cut a dash' in the company of his friends. Her younger daughter, Esther, is described as 'a little merry romp of fourteen; as honest-hearted and as guileless and simple as her sister, but with a fearless spirit of her own,' and Helen, rejoicing in this fearless spirit of Esther's, feels that her mother 'will find some difficulty in bending [her] to her purposes' (p.244). Helen enlightens Esther as to the misery she will surely endure if she consents to marry without love the unprincipled man chosen for her by her mother, who, determined to get her way, tires out her daughter by relentlessly subjecting her to 'persecutions . . . in behalf of her rejected suitor – not violent, but wearisome and unremitting like a continual dropping' (p.439). Esther, throughout all this, amazingly enough, has the will-power to remain strong in her faith and guided by Helen, to resist and finally find true love and happiness by marrying Helen's brother. We are not informed how Helen's brother has managed to escape a tainted upbringing, except for the fact that he has been brought up in the countryside away from urban temptations. Anne in emphasising Esther's resistance through strong will-power, shows, on her part, a psychological awareness of the character of Esther and young, impressionable girls like her. She is not simply saying that a Christian upbringing is sufficient in itself, but rather recognising that it is also the individual's qualities of mind and spirit and the reception of a code of strong values which dictate whether this goal is achievable or not. Anne has shown us an example in Helen's case, of such a training initially failing, possibly, as hinted at by her aunt, through some indulgence on her part towards her niece. As regards Branwell, his upbringing had also tended towards over-indulgence, yet he too had been subjected to a training in which both his father and aunt had tried to impart to him a code of morals. It was Branwell himself who had chosen to disregard their guide-lines and to go his own way. There are always two parts to the transaction. The first part implies an individual's readiness to instruct, in truly Christian fashion, and to lead by example, and the second, an individual's readiness to take in and obey the teaching offered. Rebellion lies at the heart of failure and Anne indicates how human beings continually fail through a lack of desire to choose to obey and follow such teaching. The issue of Free Will is certainly brought into play by Brontë as she depicts how some individuals, who, after receiving every advantage of upbringing, still prefer to rebel against the system and opt for their own solution. The sentiment behind the Parable of the Sower, where not all seed that is sown bears fruit, might well have been the biblical source for her examples here.

In *The Tenant of Wildfell Hall*, there are, however, fine examples where Anne's guide-lines are put into practice and do indeed result in some good parenting, such as by Mrs. Markham to Gilbert, Fergus and Rose; by Helen's aunt to her niece; and by Helen herself to her little Arthur. In the first chapter of *The Tenant,* written in the form of a letter from Gilbert Markham to the husband of his sister, Rose, Gilbert returns to events which happened in the autumn of 1827, twenty-one years prior to this letter. The date of the letter is 1848 and coincides with the date of publication of *The Tenant of Wildfell Hall,* the first of many literary contrivances which take place in this novel. The reader is introduced rapidly to a happy family, a mother, caring and interested in 'what her children have been about' (p.36) and convinced that her son, Gilbert, of twenty-four years of age, is capable of great achievements, whose father is seen to have always advocated an honest walk in life. We also meet Gilbert's sister of nineteen years of age, Rose, and a younger brother of seventeen, called Fergus. The 'excessively pretty' lady also introduced at this point is a Mrs. Graham, who is placed in a similar but slightly older age group than Gilbert but 'not above twenty-five or twenty-six years of age' possibly to distract the reader from the idea of instant match-making. Another small family is also presented to the readers, the Rev. M. Millward, father of Eliza and Mary Millward, who is always, we are told, with a touch of Anne's dry humour to cheer us on our way through her tale, very conscious of what he eats and drinks 'without being unduly abstemious'. Mr. Millward echoes Anne's thoughts on the ills of being over-indulgent to one's son, citing biblical references to Eli, David and Absalom as proof of his reflections on this subject. Yet, at the same time, we learn from Mrs. Markham, who has two sons to bring up, that she cannot readily listen to the clergyman on this subject, which proves 'galling to her feelings' and causes her to exclaim: 'I wish to goodness he had a son himself! He wouldn't be so ready with his advice to other people then; – he'd see what it is to have a couple of boys to keep in order!' By this method of presenting both sides of the issue, Anne shows us a glimpse of the truth of the situation. Indeed, Mr. Millward's occasional lapses of drinking over-copiously of Mrs. Markham's home-made wines and eating over-heartedly of her home-made food make it evident to the reader that his beliefs are being preached rather than lived out. In contrast with this way of acting, we see Mrs. Markham being portrayed as strict but kind and also 'the soul of order and punctuality'. She wants to see her children well presented before society, but, above all, cares for their welfare. Unlike Mr. Bloomfield in *Agnes Grey,* who always wants his children made 'decent', her ambition for them is based on entirely different reasons. His wish stems from selfishness and a desire not to be embarrassed before society by the appearance and actions of his annoying children, whereas hers comes from a selflessness which makes her insist on qualifying the kind of society she wants for her children as being a 'decent society' (p.50). In return for her love and affection for her family, her son, Gilbert, when describing his mother, calls her 'that honoured lady' so revealing how much she is appreciated, and how well her lessons have been absorbed by him and by the rest of her family. Her industriousness in keeping her home a warm, inviting, clean and shining place, always ready to receive guests, is not simply a façade invented by her to increase her self-importance in the eyes of society, but is much more for her own family's comfort. We see her listening intently to what her children have to recount to her over tea, and see her even managing to muster up enthusiasm for her younger son's story of badger-baiting activities. She listens to him with 'a degree of maternal admiration' which Gilbert, showing more than a hint of jealousy, suggests is 'highly disproportioned to its object!' She shows sympathy too for Mrs. Graham, mentioned over tea as a stranger to the neighbourhood, and determines to visit her to see if she can alleviate her loneliness and help her to settle in. Her qualities are indeed many and the reader feels privileged to witness such a picture of maternal love and warmth, where the older children's activities are seen to be strongly supervised by a loving mother and, in their infancy, by united parents.

Mrs. Markham is also very interested in whom her children will choose as their future partners and evidently disapproves of any possible union between Eliza Millward, the Vicar's daughter, and Gilbert, her elder son and heir to the estate. At one of his mother's parties, Gilbert snatches a kiss from Eliza Millward as she is leaving, but is observed by his mother, who shows him her disapproval, explaining at length the disadvantages of marrying a girl in whom there is 'neither beauty, nor cleverness, nor goodness, nor anything else that's desirable.' Her honesty reveals how desperately she cares about his future and wants the best possible spouse for him. This advice is grudgingly accepted by Gilbert, who reveals his good nature here and also the respect he has for his mother in that he does not react to it as interference in his affairs, but rather reluctantly accepts it as spoken out of her love for him. Mrs. Markham even manages to exact some sort of promise from him that he will think twice before marrying such a girl, letting her disapproval of Eliza be known by him through the emotive adjectives she uses to describe Eliza's flirtatious ways and dark eyes which she calls 'almost diabolically – wicked, or irresistibly bewitching'. Gilbert, although a reluctant listener, proves ready to obey her request to reflect well on the matter before making a decision. The contrast between Eliza and Rose Markham is quite striking, for Rose has been educated never to flirt or act indiscreetly and to selflessly set out to please the men folk of the family in an entirely different fashion from the more selfish approach of Eliza's. Mrs. Markham gives her recipe for happiness in a household, stating that it is a wife's business to please her husband but a man's to please himself. The reverse of this attitude is seen in *Agnes Grey*, giving rise to a very unhappy household, where Lady Ashby refuses to do anything to please her husband; instead, expecting him to please her. Mrs. Markham goes on to list what is expected of a good husband by his wife, comparing it with what her own husband, Gilbert's father, has done for her: 'He always said I was a good wife, and did my duty, and he always did his – bless him! – he was steady and punctual, seldom found fault without a reason, always did justice to my good dinners, and hardly ever spoiled my cookery by delay – and that's as much as any woman can expect of any man' (p.79). This quotation reveals the element of 'give and take' and the caring attitude on both sides, which constituted, in her eyes, the recipe for success in their marriage!

Another family scene at the Markham's follows, at which the young Mrs. Graham and her son, Arthur, are present. The slight altercations between the two mothers, Mrs. Graham and Mrs. Markham, over the former's worries at being separated from her child or at his drinking any wine, take place, before the reader (who is in the same position of unawareness of facts as Mrs. Markham) can get to know the circumstances which have caused Helen Graham to exhibit such anxiety. Indeed, all that is known at this stage is that Mrs. Markham has had a worthy husband who has been a good father to her children. It is only later on, when the full story of Helen Graham's sufferings becomes known, that Mrs. Markham can appreciate why Helen is being what she considers as over-protective to young Arthur. Helen, when questioned whether her son could not stay with the servant on her next visit rather than undertake such a long walk, replies in the negative, stating that: 'he is my only treasure, and I am his only friend, so we don't like to be separated' (p.51). Mrs. Markham, unaware of the true circumstances, calls her doting and suggests, in her plain-spoken manner, that such parenting will result in the child becoming ashamed of always being tied to his mother's apron strings. The visit progresses from bad to worse for, when young Arthur is offered wine, he refuses to drink it. Mrs. Graham then reveals to the gathered company the reason for this refusal saying that 'he detests the very sight of wine' since she has made him swallow a little wine or weak spirits and water by way of medication when he was sick. She continues by adding that she has 'done what she could to make him hate them'. Her response gives rise to merriment, but the seriousness of her attempts to justify what she has done, reveals the intensity of her feelings on this subject: 'By that means [she] hope[s] to save him from one degrading vice at least'. Indeed, she states that she wishes that she could 'render the incentives to every other equally innoxious in his case' (p.54). Mrs. Markham, who, like Anne's readers, cannot yet understand her reasoning, responds once again in an extremely honest, if not rather too forthright, a manner, telling Mrs. Graham that if she persists in this method of bringing up her child, she will turn him into the 'veriest milksop that ever was sopped' (p.54). The term 'milksop' was also used by Charlotte in *The Professor* in connection with the child, Victor. Gilbert, also unaware of Mrs. Graham's past sufferings, joins in the debate, kindly urging her not to clear the stones from her son's path but rather to teach him to walk firmly over them and so let him learn to go alone. Helen strongly reacts against Mrs. Markham's advice not to educate the boy herself by 'petting him up and slaving to indulge his follies and caprices', for she replies that to do as much would be 'criminal weakness' and that is certainly not her intent. Nor, she continues, is it her intent to send him to school, which she feels would result in his learning 'to despise his mother's authority and affection.' Here is the crux of the matter concerning love and authority. Helen, in her impassioned speech, voices Anne's fears that rebellion against authority could easily ensue if a child were to be separated from his parents and the relationship between them severed. The child could then become more intent on going his own way, which could lead to disaster and an out-and-out revolt against parental standards. An interesting debate on boys' education, with much heat on both sides, then takes place between Gilbert and Helen and the subject of girls' education is also explored, allowing the readers to learn of contemporary views on the subject and to hear, at first hand, Anne's own opposing ideas to those of her age. Mrs. Graham asks why girls have to be guarded from 'the very knowledge of evil', suggesting facetiously that Gilbert Markham might think a woman has no virtue or is 'so feeble-minded, that she cannot withstand temptation, – and though she might be pure and innocent as long as she is kept in ignorance and restraint, yet, being destitute of real virtue, to teach her how to sin is at once to make her a sinner, . . . whereas, in the nobler sex, there is a natural tendency to goodness, guarded by a superior fortitude, which, the more it is exercised by trials and dangers, is only the further developed.' (p.57) This blatantly sarcastic attack on the attitude to women of the male dominated society of her day has been placed in the mouth of a lady, who turns out in the novel to have forfeited her place in society through her own actions.

Despite the heated words, a relationship between Gilbert and young Arthur starts to build up and, in the first part of the novel, Gilbert, on more than one occasion, can be seen to act out the role of a father to Helen's son. Conscious of little Arthur's attraction to his dog, he encourages the child to play with it, so building up a relationship of trust between them. In a party at his mother's home, which Helen attends along with the child, little Arthur is even content to sit on Gilbert's lap and look at 'specimens of horses, cattle, pigs, and model farms portrayed in the volume' before him. The child is evidently at ease with Gilbert and politely refuses to leave him at his mother's request, supplying her with good reasons why he should come to her only after seeing the pictures. Indeed, his affections have undoubtedly been given to Gilbert, for, when his mother deliberately omits to shake hands with him after the contentious debate on education, it is little Arthur who reminds her to do so. When Helen does not attend the next party, Mrs. Markham mentions her views on bringing up her child to Mr. Millward who assures her, in no mean terms, that to abstain from wine is to despise one of God's gifts. Helen's brother, Mr. Lawrence, who, not yet known to the company to have any link with the so-called Mrs. Graham, is present at the same gathering and in true brotherly fashion defends Helen's case to the utmost of his ability by underlining the need for a child to avoid wine if he 'by the fault of its parents' is 'naturally prone to intemperance'. This, at last, alerts the readers as to a possible reason for Helen's extra care of her son.

Gilbert gradually builds up a relationship with Helen as her friend, and meets her occasionally on her solitary walks, admitting only to himself how much he likes talking to her and also to 'her little companion' whom he finds 'to be a very amiable, intelligent, and entertaining little fellow; and we soon became excellent friends' (p.72). Helen, on seeing the pleasure her son derives from the acquaintance, which even to her protective instincts, seems perfectly harmless, welcomes Gilbert on these terms, but on these terms alone. Gilbert is allowed to let Arthur canter or gallop along on his horse and continues to please Helen with his attentions to her son, especially when she sees that racing around with the dog, Sancho, is helping to render her child's delicate frame less so. Her confidence grows slowly in Gilbert and, on one occasion, she even allows him to take her son for a ride on a horse in a field which is only just within her range of vision.

The following May, a party, including Helen and little Arthur, sets off on an excursion to the coast with the ostensible purpose of enabling Helen, to see some new scenery as a possible subject for her paintings, for she has, by now, admitted to Gilbert that she paints to earn a living. While Helen sketches, Mary Millward is put in charge of young Arthur, which rouses Gilbert's jealousy at not being the one chosen by Helen to look after him. He is not unaware, that Helen enjoys Mary's company, and on a visit to the Vicarage has noted how similarly she and Mary feel about the rearing of children. Mary had confessed to Helen how much she approved of her views and had also revealed how much she liked children and had been so happy to find in Helen 'mammas like those who can duly appreciate their treasures' (p.72). Anne's views on rearing a child are reflected in these statements where the mother's love of her child is seen as highly commendable. They contrast starkly with the idea bandied about in her age that many mothers have no affection whatsoever for their children as is evident from Lady Ashby's statement to Agnes, in *Agnes Grey*, when she states that she finds little to interest her in her baby daughter. During this trip to the coast, it is Gilbert who fulfils a paternal role by rescuing young Arthur, when he manages to get away from Mary's care and accidentally falls over the cliff side. Naturally, Gilbert wins even more of Helen's approval for this action.

Initially, Gilbert had played with Arthur for his own sake, as he liked the child. Then, later on, he begins to play a game of tactics using his friendship with the child to win over the mother. He decides to 'first establish [his] position as a friend . . . the patron and playfellow of her son, the sober, solid, plain-dealing friend of herself' (p.93), and then to enlarge on this to gain her affections. He gives a puppy to Arthur, then a well-chosen book to herself, but this latter action causes him problems with Helen, who is willing to accept presents for her son but not for herself, as, conscious of her married state, she has no intention of being obliged to Gilbert on any score. This again causes confusion in the mind of the reader, who is unable to fathom her out or understand her reason for refusal, and whose appetite to know more is certainly whetted by this stylistic technique of Anne's of giving us the result of what has happened to her heroine before giving us the facts leading up to these events. Eventually, Gilbert persuades her to accept the gift of *Marmion* by Sir Walter Scott, but only on her own terms. Their relationship grows gradually and throughout all the ensuing attacks on her honour made by Eliza and her friend, Jane Wilson, who suspect her of a relationship with Mr. Lawrence, whom they think might well be the father of Arthur, so much does he resemble him, Gilbert continues to support her loyally. Right up until the moment Gilbert actually sees her with Mr. Lawrence, he remains adamant that she is innocent of such charges. However, after witnessing their meeting, he is overcome by doubts, so much so that it takes Helen's intervention to persuade him to read her journal, so that he (and we) may learn the truth of the situation. At this point, the novel enters a new stage, changing from being a first person narrative by Gilbert to being a first person account by Helen. Her diary entries reveal to Gilbert her past sufferings and the reasons why she brings up her child as she does. The reader now learns of her background and of the events which have led her to the isolated Wildfell Hall and at last, can understand more easily the role that this single mother is performing to the best of her ability.

As the diary unfolds, we learn of Helen's upbringing and the sound teaching she has received from her aunt, who bade Helen to receive all male attention 'coldly and dispassionately, every attention, till you have ascertained and duly considered the worth of the aspirant.' She advises her strongly against external attractions, 'flattery and light discourse' and urges her to go after principle, 'good sense, respectability, and moderate wealth' (p.150). Indeed, she warns her against marrying a handsome but worthless reprobate which is precisely what Helen does. Helen now emerges in a totally different light as we meet her in her teens, struggling to keep her promise to her aunt to marry a man of whom she can approve, respect and honour and then failing to accept her aunt's choice of suitor, Mr. Boarham, whom she finds too 'upright, honourable, sensible, sober, respectable!' Instead, Helen opts for a complete contrast to Mr. Boarham, Mr. Huntingdon, whom her aunt warns her in no mean terms is 'a bit wildish' and 'destitute of principle and prone to every vice that is common to youth' (p.153). Her aunt continues to do her best to guide Helen towards a more propitious choice telling her of the dangers of 'linking oneself to an unworthy, unprincipled partner', hinting strongly that she too had made a bad move in choosing Mr. Maxwell as her husband. Anne once again presents her readers with facts that will only become clear as later events are unfolded. It is too early for Helen to realise the truth of her aunt's statements and she remains unmoved by her advice, replying that she believes she will be capable of advising her husband and reminding him of what is right, even if he were deficient in both sense and principle. Her aunt valiantly continues in her attempts to convince her otherwise, even mentioning an intrigue Huntingdon is suspected of having had with a married lady, but Helen, whose ears appear stoppered, refuses to believe it. Her aunt, still unwilling to give up and desperate to save her niece from her impending fate if she were to marry such a man, spells out the problem as clearly as she can, stating that 'a few unprincipled mothers may be anxious to catch a young man of fortune without reference to his character; and thoughtless girls may be glad to win the smiles of so handsome a gentleman, without seeking to penetrate beyond the surface, but you, I trusted, were better informed than to see with their eyes, and judge with their perverted judgment' (p.166). Anne is here voicing her opposition to the views of her age regarding the inexperience and ignorance of females who she feels are insufficiently taught to be able to make a solid judgment regarding their future partner. In reply, Helen can only admit her fatal attraction for Arthur Huntingdon, and try to explain to her aunt that, even if she hates the sins, she loves the sinner, 'and would do much for his salvation, even supposing your suspicions to be mainly true – which I do not and will not believe' (pp.166/67). The aunt, Mrs. Maxwell, again warns Helen of the impending misery of uniting her fortunes to those of such a man, but Helen will not heed her words and remains adamant that she will 'strive to recall him to the path of virtue – God grant me success'. This attitude persists until after a departure for Staningley, which is arranged by the aunt to give Helen the opportunity to spend some time away from Huntingdon, in order to reflect more deeply on her aunt's advice and to see more clearly the folly of throwing herself away on someone so unworthy. The separation works wonders and Helen determines to refuse Huntingdon until she can discover whether her aunt's opinion or her own is nearer the truth. She even arrives at the conclusion that it is a creature of her own imagination that she loves, not Huntingdon. Unfortunately, however, at this point in time, Mr. Maxwell, her uncle, very much against his wife's wishes, invites Wilmot, Boarham and Huntingdon to come to hunt at Staningley and Helen, seeing Huntingdon again so soon after the previous meeting is lost. She consoles herself with the thoughts that by 'wise counsels and sweet, attractive goodness' (p.188), she will be able to change him. Indeed, she convinces herself that it is the fault of Arthur's 'bad, selfish, miserly father, who, to gratify his own sordid passions, restricted [Arthur] in the most innocent enjoyment of childhood and youth, and so disgusted him with every kind of restraint – and a foolish mother

who indulged him to the top of his bent, deceiving her husband for
him, and doing her utmost to encourage those germs of folly and vice
it was her duty to suppress' (pp.190/191). Anne's argument against
the attitude, prevalent in her times, of parents who are not united in
thought and show over-indulgence and lack of interest in their
children is spelt out here. She also shows how, even in the case where
a girl becomes aware of faults in her suitor, the ideas of the age allow
her to be drawn into the net of accepting him by feeding her the false
idea that she will be able to reform him. After meeting Huntingdon
this second time, Helen cannot bring herself to refuse his attentions
and is indeed drawn into a most unsuitable marriage, revealing a lack
of self-control and reason in the way she acts contrary to her religious
principles. Her aunt, does not give up even at this late stage and
warns her devout niece that Huntingdon, if he is truly vicious, will go
to Hell and therefore be parted from Helen for ever. It is at this point,
that Helen brings in Anne's views on Universal Salvation and
declares that such a separation would not be for ever but 'only till he
has paid the uttermost farthing' but that such a belief should not be
widely published for fear that some 'poor wretch would be likely to
presume upon it to his own destruction.'[15]

The aunt is not alone in fearing the union between Helen and
Arthur Huntingdon, for others join in the attack on him even Helen's
friend, Milicent Hargrave, who confesses herself deeply surprised at
Helen's choice, for as she says to her 'you are so superior to him in
every way, and there's something so bold – and reckless – about him –
so I don't know how – but I always feel a wish to get out of his way,
when I see him approach.' Milicent continues by saying that 'there's
nothing noble or lofty in his appearance' and even remarking that his
face is too red (p.195), another advance mention by Anne to aid the
readers to realise how heavily Huntingdon drinks. Milicent softens
the blow by saying it had been her wish that Helen would marry her
brother, Walter, whom she felt was much nicer and better than Mr.
Huntingdon in every way. Unfortunately, Helen latches onto this as
being the real reason why Milicent has spoken against Arthur and
ignores her friend's words of warning just as she has ignored her
aunt's. Yet another incident occurs before the marriage which might
well have served as proof of Arthur's bad character, if Helen had been
willing to accept it as such. Arthur relates to her at length how it is he
who aided the fall of Lord Lowborough, who has been forced to shrink
from his company 'fearing lest I should wile him back to destruction'
in 'that devil's den' (pp.209/210). Huntingdon even admits to Helen
that at one time, he pursued Annabella Wilmot but left her for Helen,
whom he feels is a brighter treasure. Whether this is true is
questionable, as Annabella undoubtedly had the larger fortune, but

evidently wanted desperately, as did Rosalie Murray in *Agnes Grey*, a title to go with it, and therefore chose to marry a man she despised, rather than Huntingdon, to whom she would have given as much as she received. Lowborough, Arthur recounts, is now happy at his good fortune in obtaining the hand in marriage of Annabella Wilmot and has told Huntingdon that he is no longer a 'castaway', a term evidently taken from Cowper's poem of the same name, a poet beloved by Anne, and having as its meaning one who is cast ashore after a shipwreck, and also one deserted by God and consequently unsaved, as Cowper and Branwell Brontë considered themselves to be. Helen is aghast at these revelations but even more upset at Huntingdon's refusal to tell Lowborough that Annabella is marrying him just for his 'title and pedigree', and 'that delightful old family seat.' She cannot understand how Huntingdon can mock another person's sufferings, but still refuses to break off her engagement to him, even though her trusted servant, Rachel, tells her that the servants have been talking a great deal of the goings on of both Lord Lowborough and of her beloved fiancé. Perhaps, it is rather too late in the day to do so, as young ladies who jilted their suitors were very much frowned upon in the nineteenth century, as can be seen in Elizabeth Gaskell's *Wives and Daughters,* where Cynthia jilts two of her suitors before finally marrying another, much to the disgust of society.

A gap of ten weeks ensues before the wedding takes place and Helen, although she loves his affectionate letters, is beginning to wonder whether he can ever be truly serious or write or speak to her in solid earnest. She says, 'I don't much mind now; but if it be always so, what shall I do with the serious part of myself?' (p.214), but does nothing to pursue this line of questioning. Perhaps her pride will not allow her at this late stage to admit she has made a mistake. In any case, the realisation of this comes very quickly after her wedding, for eight weeks into marriage, she recognises that she could easily have known his faults if she had been willing to listen 'for everyone was willing enough to tell me about him, and he himself was no accomplished hypocrite, but I was wilfully blind' (p.215). Here Anne is not so much pointing out a lack of moral guidance during Helen's infancy, which we have seen was certainly not the case, but rather her lack of self-control and her wilful pride which are revealed in this emotional entanglement with Arthur. If she had been obedient to her aunt and listened to her advice, this could never have come about. The selection of a marriage partner is shown to be one of Anne's main areas of concern, for once united to a man, a wife was unable to extricate herself from the partnership and incapable of being in control of any parental relationships. The law of the land was adamant, and divorce by a woman of her husband simply did not take place.

Arthur initially treats Helen like a frail butterfly seeming fearful of exposing her to society in case she is changed by it, but later goes on to upset her with his jealousy of her devotion to God, refusing to listen to her advice when she talks seriously to him about his lack of faith. Her requests that he try to think more deeply and to fortify himself against the temptation to call evil good, and good evil, result in their having a protracted quarrel lasting four days, which includes the well-known episode of her shutting her bedroom door and refusing her favours to her husband – a revolutionary move for Victorian days! Yet Helen still retains some hope that she may change Arthur for the good and that they will be 'happy again in spite of [her] aunt's forebodings and [her] own unspoken fears' (p.229).

Arthur now frequently practises deception on Helen by claiming the need to go off to London on business. On one occasion, Helen manages to deter him from going alone and they leave together. Helen learns of the impending marriage of Milicent with one of Arthur's 'friends', Mr. Hattersley, and is asked by Milicent for advice as to what to do for she is not at all happy with the way things have developed and the fact that she is, more or less, being forced by her mother into marrying Hattersley. This wrings the confession from Helen that 'it is better to make a bold stand now, though at the expense of disappointing and angering both mother and brother, and lover, than to devote your whole life, hereafter, to misery and vain regret' (p.232). However, Milicent is not strong enough to resist the pressure from her mother, who clearly intends to marry her daughters to anyone with money!

Although Helen is compelled to return home from her London visit after only one month away from home, Arthur does not come back for a full three and a half months. On his return, Helen decides to be kindness itself to him and to 'shame him into virtue' by spoiling him with her gentle attentions. This treatment is proved to work no better than the over-indulgence of his mother, for, one month later, Arthur, having completely recovered from the effects of his licentious behaviour, is 'as lusty and reckless, as light of heart and head as ever, and as restless and hard to amuse as a spoilt child.' Despite all Helen's efforts, she fails miserably to change her husband. Arthur has 'no more idea of exerting himself to overcome obstacles than he has of restraining his natural appetites, these two things are the ruin of him. Helen lays 'them both to the charge of his harsh yet careless father and his madly indulgent mother' and tells us her ideas on how a mother should cope as a parent: 'If ever I am a mother I will zealously strive against this crime of over-indulgence – I can hardly give it a milder name when I think of the evils it brings' (pp.237-238). Anne here reiterates the warning she issued in her first novel about the dangers of a parent like Mrs. Murray, who has never had any durable relationship with her children and has urged her governess never to let them exert themselves in any way, so denying them in one fell swoop both education and useful occupations. We witness the sad result of such parenting in her daughter, Lady Ashby, who, having made a disastrous marriage, fortunately realises what her mother's lack of guide-lines and information have meant in her own life, and determines that she will make some efforts to ensure that her baby girl, given sufficient care and attention, will turn out better than she has done.

It does not take very long for Helen to realise the terrible mistake she has made in marrying Huntingdon. We see her male parallel in Lord Lowborough who, although married only eight months, also finds himself in bad humour at his wife's 'reckless disregard of principle that makes him bitterly regret that she is not as good as she is charming and beloved.' Helen, sensing that his despair is similar to her own, pities him from her heart, for as she says, she knows 'the misery of such regrets' (p.241). Lowborough, because of having been drawn into bad company through his initial ignorance of where it would lead him, can be compared, in some ways, with Helen, who herself fell through wilfulness, for she had been sheltered by her aunt from those excesses to which Lowborough, as a boy and later a man, had been subjected. Both are noble characters and share high principles, innate goodness, and a strong belief in a Christian code of morals, and, in their fall, are depicted by Anne as typifying human frailty, serving to help illustrate God's mercy in forgiving all sinners.

Once her child is born, Helen becomes very aware of 'how strong are a parent's temptations to spoil an only child' and struggles to keep a balance in her treatment of little Arthur during her husband's frequent absences from home. She worries ceaselessly about the effects on her child of her husband's lascivious behaviour and is anxious to instruct him 'to respect his father and yet to avoid his example.' The basis for such a sentiment again stems from Anne's great knowledge of the Bible, and is a reference to 2 Corinthians 6 verse 14:

'Do not be yoked together with unbelievers. For what do righteousness and wickedness have in common? Or what fellowship can light have with darkness?'

This constitutes a dilemma for any wife in a marriage where the partner, as here, does not share Christian views and Helen, now convinced of Arthur's lack of faith, cannot reconcile herself to his definition of what is expected of a wife, for he maintains that a wife 'is a thing to love one devotedly and to stay at home – to wait upon her husband, and amuse him and minister to his comfort in every possible way, while he chooses to stay with her; and, when he is absent, to attend to his interests, domestic or otherwise, and patiently wait his return; no matter how he may be occupied in the meantime' (pp.256-258). She would have had no difficulty in ministering to his every comfort, but could not go along with the idea of accepting that it was of no matter to a wife should her husband be engaged in evil practices. In other words, Arthur felt that he could act in any way he pleased but that Helen was to act out her part as his 'household deity' (p.280), again reminiscent of the Victorian idealisation of wives in their homes. Anne voices her views through Helen that marriage is the union of two souls, which explains clearly, in view of Arthur's behaviour, why she often felt 'debased, contaminated by the union', even to the point of becoming 'familiarized with vice and almost a partaker in his sins.' Helen had, by now, realized the gravity of her mistake in allying herself with such a man, and blames her vain presumption: 'Fool that I was to dream that I had strength and purity enough to save myself and him! Such vain presumption would be rightly served, if I should perish with him in the gulf from which I sought to save him' (p.274). This reflection of Anne's own worries during her days with the Robinson family, where she witnessed the corruption of her brother, can also be felt in *Agnes Grey,* where Agnes expresses her fears at being corrupted by the lack of goodness around her whilst working with the Murray girls. Anne seeks to warn her readers not to mix with those who would lead them into evil dealings, for fear that they too become contaminated by their actions and conversation. This concept is once again based on Anne's knowledge of the Bible, 1 Corinthians 15 verses 33-34:

> 'Do not be misled: Bad company corrupts good character.
> Come back to your senses as you ought, and stop sinning;
> for there are some who are ignorant of God – I say this to
> your shame.'

Arthur goes off to stay in Scotland, this time with Walter Hargrave, and gives his wife permission meanwhile to visit her Uncle and Aunt Maxwell at Staningley, where she endeavours to conceal from her aunt much of what has been going on. Her desire is to preserve her aunt, whom she calls her best friend, 'from the slightest participation in those sorrows, from which she had striven so hard to save me.' Helen admits to herself how tenderly her aunt had reared her from infancy, 'so carefully guided and instructed in childhood and youth' and feels intensely guilty at the disappointment she has caused to her aunt's hopes. Again, there is a hint of a seeming parallel between Helen's uncle and Huntingdon. Both men had belonged to a band of corrupt men. The aunt evidently realizes how much Helen is suffering, perhaps because she too has lived through similar times, and comforts her niece as she leaves for Grassdale, advising her not to spoil her child 'to gratify your present feelings, it will be too late to repent it when your heart is broken.' This implies that this is what she did with little Helen and that her heart is indeed broken by what has happened to her niece. Indeed, it seems very likely that the aunt's rearing of Helen was often hindered by her husband, who, if one judges him by his friends, has evidently not supported her attempts to bring up her niece in a Godly way. This unhappy cycle of events continues in Helen's life, where little Arthur's upbringing is certainly being affected by the actions of his untrustworthy father. This causes her great concern over the effect such actions are having on her child's character. Helen, conscious of her aunt's heartbreak in being unable to prevent her niece from following in her own footsteps, is even more determined to succeed with her own son.

Indeed, the novel reveals what good and loving parents both Helen and Milicent make, as we see when Milicent too has a child, and the two friends, often together, play with their children and spend time building up a solid and loving relationship with them. In fact, they romp 'with the little creatures, almost as merry and wild as themselves.' Both wives know the sadness of having married a corrupt man and are apprehensive for Esther, Milicent's sister, that the influence of her mother and of the artful governess, engaged to look after her, will succeed in forcing Esther to marry against her better judgment. Milicent rejoices that Esther spends a great deal of time with Helen, and urges her friend to impress on her young sister 'never, on any account, or for anybody's persuasion, to marry for the sake of money, or rank, or establishment, or any earthly thing, but true affection and well-grounded esteem' (pp.292-293). As per usual, instead of adopting a heavy, didactic pose, Anne is illustrating the problem by the way in which her fictional heroines live it out.

Helen's marital situation deteriorates even more when she discovers for herself that her husband is not only misbehaving whilst absent from the house, but is actually committing adultery with her so-called friend, Annabella Lowborough, in their own garden shrubbery. This scene could well have been influenced by the testimony of the Robinsons' gardener, who reported Branwell's misbehaviour with his employer's wife, to her husband, and was responsible for Branwell's dismissal from the Robinson household in 1845.[16] This horrible proof of something Helen had feared but not known for certain is more than she feels able to bear and she turns to God for help, feeling refreshed after her prayers, and courageous enough to speak to Arthur of the situation, even asking him for his permission to leave the household and go away with their child, with or without the little fortune remaining to her! Arthur, representative here of the oppression of the age, refuses vehemently and Helen is compelled to live out the life of misery, which she knows she has brought on herself. Her husband's refusal to let her go her own way is worsened by her decision to live in the same house but separate from him, evidently a sensible choice under the circumstances but also an incredibly daring idea for the times. From then on, Helen is forced to watch how her husband spitefully turns his attention on their child, wilfully trying to hurt her by thwarting all her attempts to bring up little Arthur without indulgence. Painfully, she notes the effect on her child and how, as she says, he is beginning to note the division in his parents' views: 'If I attempt to curb his will, or look gravely on him for some act of childish disobedience, he knows his other parent will smile and take his part against me,' most probably what she herself had been subjected to as a child with her uncle and aunt. She begins to long for her husband's absences, during which time she does her best to overcome the vices Arthur has introduced to their child, and to change little Arthur from being 'a selfish, disobedient and mischievous boy' in whom his father is 'preparing the soil for those vices he has so successfully cultivated in his own perverted nature' (p.333) into the good little boy she so longs to raise. It is intimated too that this is what happened to Lord Lowborough as a child, causing him to turn out as he did. Anne paints him more sympathetically than she does Huntingdon for, once conscious of his errors, Lowborough strives to reform himself and to succeed only through his reliance on God and his sheer will-power in combating the evils to which he was so sorely attracted. Lowborough emerges from his experiences desperate to live by a strongly biblical code of practice, as can be seen from the way he later brings up his children. The scene in which he chides Helen for not telling him sooner of his wife's adultery with Huntingdon reveals the strength of his resolve, for, although he is depicted by his so-called friends as an object of scorn for refusing to fight a duel with Huntingdon, his reasons for not complying with their suggestion are clearly seen to come not from cowardice but rather from the force of his convictions that it is for God alone to avenge his foes. His separation from Annabella ensues and he decides to live in strict seclusion in his old castle in the north. This is purposely engineered through his own efforts in order to give protection to his children, of whom the son is his own, but the little girl a product of Huntingdon's and Annabella's illicit union, for she has the blue eyes and light auburn hair of her father. Lowborough is kind enough to accept her as his own and to keep her 'from conscientious motives alone, thinking it wrong to abandon her to the teaching and example of such a woman as her mother' (p.354). In Annabella's case, the results of unbridled indulgence in her childhood continue to take their toll upon her. Never contradicted when young, she becomes unstoppable on her path of sin as she grows older, where deceit and adultery mean nothing to her, for her self-absorption allows her only to appreciate wild enjoyment.

Lowborough's attempts at bringing up his two children are quite different from what we see going on in the Huntingdon household, where Arthur and his band of merry men continue to encourage little Arthur to indulge 'in all the embryo vices a little child can show, and to instruct [him] in all the evil habits he could acquire – in a word, to 'make a man of him' was one of their staple amusements (p.386). The child becomes confused by the treatment he receives from his father and the opposing treatment he receives from his mother. As young as he is, although he enjoys the merriment he causes to his father and friends, at the same time, he is pained, to see his mother's reaction to his actions and asks: 'Mamma, why don't you laugh?' and plaintively calling on his father, 'Make her laugh, papa – she never will' (p.386). The child, becoming more and more influenced by his father's habits, gradually begins to resent his mother's attempts to force him away from his ever-merry father and friends, considering it cruel and unjust on her part, that she wants to separate him from a father who pays him such a lot of attention. Unfortunately, this sentiment of the child is fuelled to the utmost by his father, who rejoices at making Helen sit alone in her room, where she is conscious of what is going on downstairs, and, consumed with worry, constantly racks her brains for any remedy to this evil.

Finally, Helen, having reached the point at which she is unable to bear any longer the corruption of her child decides to flee abroad to New England, where she can continue to paint to earn a living. Anne now shows us the normally private Helen sharing her ideas on escaping with the scheming Hargrave, and, completely uncharacteristically for her, revealing all her plans to a man in whom she has no trust. Is this sheer desperation on her part at having no one else to whom to turn? Her uncle and aunt cannot be approached and her brother is distant from her at the time. This leads to a very awkward scene, which is misinterpreted by Grimsby, where Hargrave beseeches her to accept his protection, by which he implies her compliance to much more. Helen manages to elicit a reluctant apology from Hargrave in front of Grimsby, in which he states that his advances towards Helen had indeed been unsolicited and refused by her. Another uncharacteristic request follows when Helen, evidently confused and desperate for help, asks Hattersley to defend her honour in this matter, a task which he (also uncharacteristically and perhaps, in so doing, offering the reader an anticipation of his reform), accepts. Her defenders being corrupt themselves, the reader cannot hold out much hope of success. The attempt fails and Helen is compelled to go on parenting her son in as wise a fashion as she can muster. One example of this occurs when young Arthur is questioning his mother as to why she is so wicked – a thought placed in his mind by his father. Instead of losing her temper and instantly blaming her husband for influencing the child in this way, she talks gently to her son and reasons with him, until she can lead him to the realization that it is his papa who is wicked and not she. She does not do this in a vindictive way, but rather to help the child to grow up knowing the truth of the situation. Naturally, little Arthur is moved to tears at the thought of his beloved papa being so bad, especially as he has been taught previously by his mother that wicked people go to Hell.

Shortly after all this, Huntingdon discovers his wife's plans to escape by looking over her shoulder at what she is writing in her diary. As a result of this, he insists on taking away her money, jewellery and even her painting materials, commanding his housemaid to inform Benson, one of the servants, to burn the offending easel and stretcher. Although Arthur's intervention puts back Helen's project for quite a while, her desire to leave him remains firm and she takes comfort in the thought that the life of poverty she will lead once she has left him will mean nothing to her 'when compared with a whole eternity of peace'. Huntingdon, desperate for entertainment, eventually decides to go away to join his friends and, at last, she has a brief respite with her beloved child. She makes good progress with her son by dint of her efforts to eradicate the bad habits acquired from his father's tuition, to such a point that 'bad language seldom defiles his mouth' (p.375). She says: 'I exerted all my powers to eradicate the weeds that had been fostered in his infant mind, and sow again the good seed they had rendered unproductive.' She also succeeds in giving him 'an absolute disgust for all intoxicating liquors', which she hopes will be impossible for anyone to overcome. Helen worries that vices can be passed on from father to son, for she remembers her own father's predilection to alcohol, which, coupled with young Arthur's own father's fondness for drink, might well prove a difficult vice for the child to overcome. Her plan of surreptitiously introducing a small quantity of tartar-emetic in each glass of wine the child drank, and making him slightly nauseous and depressed after drinking it, at last convinces young Arthur that he hates all alcohol and never wishes to taste it again.

Helen's second plan of escape now begins to take shape. She decides to go to the Hall where she and her brother were born and where their mother died. She will take on her maiden name, living in one or two of its rooms on the earnings her brother can secure for her in negotiating the sale of her pictures. In the first instance, she will borrow money from him and determines to pay him back gradually, to appease her sense of honour, even though her brother has not requested repayment. We learn of his imminent visit to Grassdale and realize how the details of Helen's escape are going to be worked out. We also learn that young Arthur really does resemble her brother physically and that her brother has escaped the consequences of a similar upbringing to that of Huntingdon by simply not living in society and not mingling with such friends (p.377).

While Helen waits for the opportune moment to be able to leave, she uses her time fruitfully in encouraging her young protégée, Esther, not to accept the marriage proposal of Mr. Oldfield, a rich but perverse suitor who entirely meets with her mother's approval. Esther's mother even resorts to the deceitful suggestion that her daughter's refusal will displease Helen, but Helen and Milicent manage to make it clear to Esther that they support her in her firm stand and her rejection of any suitor whom she does not love or respect. With her sister and her friend mentally and emotionally standing beside her, Esther feels sure she will be able to resist her mother's and brother's attempts to force her to marry. Esther is only eighteen years of age and naturally needs reassurance from Helen that her decision will not make her a burden on her mother or jeopardize her brother's future by her having to stay longer at home to wait a while for the right suitor to present himself. These are evidently taunts that are already beginning to come her way. Yet, Esther's awareness of Helen's unhappiness with Huntingdon helps her to comprehend the dangers she will face if she yields and gives her sufficient knowledge of such a union to enable her to tell her friend that, if she were ever to marry, she would expect her husband to 'have no pleasures but what he shares with' her (p.380).

Before the moment of her departure arrives, Helen also tries to help Hattersley, Milicent's husband, who has begun to grow weary of Arthur's debauched conduct, by offering him wise advice to begin a new life in which he can behave 'with all decency and sobriety, as a Christian, and the father of a family should do' (p.382). He vows to reform and Helen praises his decision and is not afraid to stand up to him in support of Milicent, even showing him one or two of his wife's letters to her in a sincere attempt to convince him to change his ways. Ralph Hattersley, intent on starting off anew with his wife, openly thanks Helen for her intervention, saying to his delighted wife: 'Thank her, it's her doing!' (p.386). Hattersley's remarks speak for Anne in informing her public as to what she feels the father of a family should indeed be like – decent and sober.

Unfortunately, all is not positive as another major development occurs when Huntingdon returns home, bringing with him a governess/mistress, Miss Myers. She is portrayed as coming from the normal milieu for a governess, being the daughter of a clergyman, but is very different from Anne's first example, Agnes Grey. She does not have the excellent moral qualities of an Agnes. In addition, she has only mediocre qualifications. However, Helen suspects correctly that she has been chosen not least for her very beautiful singing voice which evidently pleases Huntingdon greatly. In bringing such a person back to his home, Huntingdon is certainly not considering his son's or his wife's welfare. Doubtless, Huntingdon wants, out of sheer vindictiveness, to hurt Helen even more by taking the charge of educating her child away from her and thereby robbing her of forming any relationship with her son. Indeed, except for the difference in gender, this illustration of Miss Myers, the daughter of a curate, employed to teach young Arthur, and seduced by Huntingdon, mirrors the position occupied by Branwell, also the son of a clergyman, at the Robinsons', where he, tutor to the Robinsons' son, was seduced by the lady of the house. The servants, especially Rachel, are very upset for their mistress and supply her with detailed intelligence of what is going on between Huntingdon and Miss Myers. Helen, unable to bear the situation any longer, writes in haste to warn Frederick that her arrival at the Hall, accompanied only by her child and servant, Rachel, is imminent. She also writes to Esther, Milicent and to her aunt forewarning them that they can only contact her in the future through her brother. Collusion between the servants and herself helps her to manage to send off her few possessions in advance, corded by the trusty Benson and sent in a cart to M– coach-office in the name of Mrs. Graham. At last, she sets off, having managed to escape without discovery, for her diary reveals that by 24 October, she is 'free and safe at last' (p.394). Her new abode is no palace as much repair work is needed, but her wing has been prepared well enough for her by her brother and Helen is more than content to take up residence there. Rachel has managed to pack a few of Helen's completed paintings, including one of Huntingdon when Helen first fell in love with him. This sets the scene for this portrait to be seen by Gilbert Markham on one of his visits to the Hall. Apparently, Helen uses it to compare her son's features with those of his father as he grows, possibly noting any growing resemblance to the weakness of his gaze. Huntingdon, distraught by her escape, for once really exerts himself to find his missing wife and son, even offering through Helen's brother the possibility of Helen being allowed to live alone on an allowance – as Annabella does – so long as she will give him back his son. His previous treachery and deceit oblige her not to trust him, and, in any case, her reason for fleeing his household is to enable young Arthur to be properly brought up in Christian fashion, away from Arthur's corruptive influence. It is at this point that her diary is interrupted and Gilbert is left longing to know what Helen has said about him on the pages she has torn out, before handing him her diary to read.

This third part of the novel changes narrator yet again, and reverts to Gilbert's account in the letter to Halford, his sister Rose's husband. Gilbert, having finished reading the Journal, gains entry to Wildfell Hall to see Helen for one last time, much to Rachel's displeasure and to young Arthur's delight. Helen allows him this final interview but, on entering her room, he can see in her face that 'a violent conflict between reason and passion was silently passing within' (p.404). This is the conflict experienced by every woman who wants desperately to follow her passion, against her better judgment, and illustrates quite vividly Anne's support for the emphasis given in the eighteenth century on sense rather than on sensibility, on reasoning and self-control rather than on yielding to one's passions. Helen tells Gilbert that in six months' time, he will hear of her precise whereabouts through her brother and that he can then write to her and she will answer him, but that they will never meet again face to face except in Heaven. After this dramatic meeting, Gilbert is moved to apologise to Helen's brother, Frederick Lawrence, for having struck him, on mistakenly thinking him guilty of a relationship with Helen. Lawrence forgives him and a rapport between them is forged, based not just on Helen, the common denominator, but also on the increasing pleasure Gilbert finds in Frederick's society, to such an extent that he even finds he is able to advise Frederick strongly against marrying Jane Wilson, advice which Frederick reluctantly accepts. Gilbert's motives are akin to those of Helen's in her attempts at advising Esther, for he, just like her, wishes to preserve his friend 'from that fatal mistake'. The novel moves on rapidly and Markham, having learnt from Eliza Millward that Helen has returned to her husband, visits Lawrence to establish the facts. He discovers that Huntingdon is very ill and that Helen, out of a sense of duty, has agreed to return home to nurse him back to health.

Once at home, Helen uses the situation to her advantage by refusing to allow her husband a visit from his child until he has signed a document, in the presence of her servant, Rachel, as witness, which places the child under her sole protection. This reveals Anne's approval of women's independence in such situations, which was in total opposition to what would have been allowed by Victorian society. Such a fearless action could well have been inspired by her reading of Wollstonecraft's *The Wrongs of Woman*, where Wollstonecraft emphasises her stand on women's rights, but with a far more political flavour than Anne's. Anne, by including such features as Helen's refusal of sexual favours to her husband, the flight with her child away from home, and then this incredibly sensitive demand for sole supervision of the child, incurred a great deal of controversy and criticism when *The Tenant* was published. Huntingdon reluctantly signs his acceptance of her conditions as he is desperate to see his child, but is clearly disappointed when he does see him, as he discovers that his previous hold over little Arthur is no more. In true paranoiac fashion, he chides Helen for prejudicing his son against him. Helen replies truthfully, telling him that, although she has not done this, she cannot deny that she would like the child to forget him and 'especially to forget the lessons you taught him' (p.432). Many separated parents today might say the same.

Through Markham's requests for information from the letters Helen sends to Lawrence, the reader learns of her progress with Huntingdon and how she has succeeded in obtaining the right to leave him whenever she wishes. During her stay at Grassdale, Helen manages to meet Esther at a crucial time when her spirit has almost been broken by the unremitting persecutions of her mother. Helen manages to give her young friend sufficient encouragement to resist the pressure upon her. Anne allows us to glimpse a possible happy future outcome for Esther by dropping her readers the hint that she wishes someone worthy of possessing Esther would come along, ending her statement with the suggestive, 'don't you, Frederick?' (p.440).

We learn too of Eliza's marriage to a wealthy tradesman of L– and of Mary Millward's marriage to Richard Wilson, who becomes the Rev. R. Wilson of the Vicarage of Lindenhope after the Rev. M. Millward's death, and also that Jane Wilson, Lawrence's former interest, is still unmarried and living alone. Markham continues to visit Lawrence to get news of Helen and learns of Huntingdon's many 'imprudences' as Helen terms them, such as his resolve to drink 'the strongest wine in the cellar' just to show her 'he would have no more humbug'. As the time passes, Huntingdon becomes increasingly ill as a result of his inability to accept Helen's and his doctor's well-meant advice to restrict his intake of alcohol, which is rapidly poisoning him to death. Helen, in order to devote more time to Huntingdon on his sick-bed, is even obliged to give her son into Esther Hargrave's charge, as her presence is constantly demanded by her husband. The relationship between young Arthur and his mother is evidently very strong, for he begs to stay with her but she, unable to bear the thought of subjecting him to his father's excessive suffering and dreadful language, feels compelled to refuse her child's request.

On one occasion, Helen manages to reach Huntingdon over the question of where he would go if he were to die without repenting, but, as he refuses to contemplate death at all, she fails yet again to convince him of the need for him to make his peace with God. Hattersley, now reformed, visits his old friend, a living proof, as it were, of Anne's views that everything is possible with God, and that, even though the majority of men remain unchanged by their wives' efforts, there can always be an exception to the rule. Hattersley even suggests sending for a clergyman, but Huntingdon cannot bring himself to turn to God for consolation and wants only Helen at his side. He feels safe if she is near, and believes his wife is saintly and that her presence can benefit him more than could that of a vicar or curate. Mortification soon sets in, freeing him of his intense pain, but frightening him when the doctor informs him that there is no longer any hope left for his survival. Helen writes 'no words can describe his anguish' (p.449). Huntingdon still refuses all the consolation she can offer him and yet clings to her 'as if [she] could save him from the fate he dreads' (p.450), unable to bring himself to repent of his former actions, and only able to fear the consequences of an after-life. Yet, at least, he now regrets having harmed his 'Nell' because of her goodness to him. However, there is no improvement in his attitude to repentance after all her attempts, except, as she says, 'He does not now, as formerly, laugh these blessed truths to scorn, but still he cannot trust, or will not comprehend them' (p.451). His last words to Helen are a request to her to pray for him. After his death, when Helen relates in her letter to Frederick what has happened, Anne's own passionate voice emerges, ringing out not only with Helen's but also with her own cry for hope, for uppermost in her mind might well have been the fate of her brother, Branwell, hastening at that present time to his death, and of her somewhat heretical sister, Emily: 'How could I endure to think that that poor trembling soul was hurried away to everlasting torment? it would drive me mad! But thank God – I have hope – not only from a vague dependence on the possibility that penitence and pardon might have reached him at the last, but from the blessed confidence, that through whatever purging fires the erring spirit may be doomed to pass – whatever fate awaits it, still, it is not lost, and God who hateth nothing that He hath made, will bless it in the end!' (p.452). Anne often took part in the bedside vigils beside her brother and, whilst writing this novel, was witnessing his debasement, seeing him, like her fictional hero, brought low by his own abuse and close to death. He died in the September of that same year, 1848, in which her novel was published. Her doctrine of Universal Salvation offered her and her public the means of keeping sane when faced by the departure of beloved family members who were unsure of their faith, fictionalised in her hero who refused to repent right up to his last breath.

As Frederick Lawrence leaves to visit Helen to help her organize her husband's funeral, Markham gives him no message and says nothing of his love for Helen as he waves off his friend. Lawrence can see nothing but gravity in Markham's expression, for Markham hides his emotions from him, thinking, out of regard for the promise he has made to Helen not to contact her before six months had elapsed and also from social etiquette, that it was not the moment to declare himself. Lawrence's prolonged absence increases Markham's doubts as to his eligibility as Helen's suitor and he dwells on the disparity of their situations. However, as a man of honour, he preserves 'a stoic calmness' throughout all this. Then another death occurs, that of her Uncle Maxwell, 'a worthless old fellow' but one who had always shown 'more kindness and affection to her than to any other creature, and she had always been accustomed to regard him as a parent' (p.457). Even here, we see the influence of the biblical precept of honouring parents, which is made much of by Anne, for Helen's uncle, although called worthless, is still loved and honoured by her at his death. Markham's 'stupidity' and 'foolish pride', adjectives he attributes to himself after the event, prevent him from slipping a letter to Lawrence for Helen on his departure to Grassdale, and once Helen moves to Staningley, whose address is unknown to him, he cannot find out how to overcome this deterrent. Meanwhile, Lowborough divorces Annabella, perfectly possible this way round, and forces himself, as a good Christian father, to treat both his son and his 'nominal daughter' 'with paternal kindness'. Anne gives him a second chance, as she does with Helen, and we hear that he remarries an older lady of 'good sense, unswerving integrity, active piety, warm-hearted benevolence, and a fund of cheerful spirits' who becomes 'an excellent mother to the children and an invaluable wife to his lordship' (pp.460-461). These qualities which Anne promotes for the ideal wife are seen to be superior, in her eyes, to remarkable beauty or wealth, although, as in *Agnes Grey*, her relatively plain heroine secretly longs for beauty on one occasion.

In the December, Markham learns of an impending marriage between Helen and Mr. Hargrave. Ever the mistress of suspense, Anne arranges this mistake to unnerve not only Markham but also her readers as the prospect of such a marriage looms large. Urged on by his fears, Markham sets off at once for Grassdale, arriving just in time to see a wedded couple emerge from the parish church. With great relief, we learn that it is Frederick Lawrence who has married Esther Hargrave, whose letter to Markham had not been received by him. Markham hears Esther sob out a wish at her wedding that her dear Helen might find such happiness as she has. Markham blesses her inwardly for her thoughts and makes his way to Grassdale, taking comfort that such a large estate was 'entailed upon little Arthur' (p.472) rather than on Helen. Knowing Helen was in Staningley, he makes his way there, caring sufficiently for his mother to write and reassure her of his movements whilst en route: 'excellent son that I was' (p.474). He finds out on the way in the coach that Staningley has been willed to Helen by her uncle, and feeling sick at the thought that, by inheriting such an enormous estate, Helen has become far outside his reach socially and financially, he determines to complete his journey, see her home and then say goodbye for ever to his dream of marrying her. Anne is intent on drawing similarities of character between Helen and Gilbert, revealing here that Gilbert's desire to marry her is not at all for mercenary reasons. As in all good romances, Helen's carriage passes by just at the propitious moment, as he is walking near her drive-way and her delighted son, on sighting him, warns his mother of Gilbert's presence. Gilbert hears Helen call out for the carriage to stop and is invited into the house, where he meets her aunt, who leaves them alone together long enough to give Helen sufficient time to overcome Markham's 'false delicacy and pride'. Helen's rather obvious wooing tactics work extremely well and Gilbert cannot resist her indirect marriage proposal through the Romantic device of offering him a rose as a symbol of her love. Important parentally, the bond between Markham and little Arthur is still very much alive as is seen when Arthur happily agrees to examine a book with him, which Helen had deliberately sent him off to fetch. Markham, honest as ever, recognizes his affection for the little chap was partially because he was Helen's son and therefore could be regarded as his own. Happily, their marriage takes place and we learn that Helen and Gilbert make good parents for the little Arthur, who, once grown, marries and lives very happily with the 'merry little Helen Hattersley', named after his mother in gratitude for her advice to Hattersley. This is evidently included in the novel so as to foster in the reader the idea that the Christian code of morals would also be adhered to by the young Arthur and little Helen, brought up as they were by such parents. Markham takes readily to Helen's aunt, who lives with them at Staningley until she dies, treating her happiness as dearly as that of his own mother, who finds it initially difficult to accept his choice of bride and his leaving Linden Grange for such a distant place. Helen shows her kindness and goodness towards Mrs. Markham, helping her to overcome her prejudice towards her and, in time, Mrs. Markham accepts the situation fully and is, at last, conscious of her son's good fortune. The novel ends at Staningley on 10 June 1847 with Fergus's engagement to the eldest daughter of a vicar. We also learn that the union of Helen and Gilbert is indeed a happy one 'blessed as they were with many promising young scions' growing up about them.

Helen now has many more chances of using the valuable experience she already has gained by rearing young Arthur 'to guide him along the perilous path of youth and train him to be God's servant while on earth, a blessed and honoured saint in heaven' (p.252). With Markham at her side, her task will no longer be an onerous one and Anne leaves us in little doubt that she will hold firm to her definition of the relationship she seeks between parent and child, who will ever be, as she says, 'my comfort and my joy, and me to be his shield, instructor, friend.'

Anne's ideas on parenting, as expressed in both her novels, do not just extend to the parents' involvement with their child, but also, as we have seen, to the child's attitude towards the parent. Markham's deference towards his mother and towards Helen's aunt is all part of the process of observing the Christian code of ethics that Anne is advocating to her public. Conscious of how much her own father has suffered through Branwell's increasing sickness, Anne endeavours to show, in this her second novel, how vital it is for all in the position of parents, to honour their commitment to their children so as to be honoured in their turn.

Chapter Four:

Background, upbringing and personal experience as inspirational sources

Much of Anne's inspiration on the subject of parenting comes from her memories of an infancy spent within a family which sincerely upheld Christian values; from her own thoughts on religion and the development of her unorthodox doctrine of Universal Salvation; from what she gleaned from parishioners' and friends' visits to her father at Haworth Parsonage and from those visits she herself made to her godparents, friends and relatives; and lastly, from her experience as a governess, when she saw, with her own eyes, how her two sets of employers and their friends lived and governed their children.

Influence of her background, upbringing and schooling

As regards the first source of inspiration, her family background, the quotation 'le milieu produit l'écrivain' (p.96) from Jean-Paul Sartre's *Qu'est-ce que la littérature?* fits in well here, revealing how Anne's background is indeed a powerful influence on both herself and her writings. It might be as well to recall that she was brought up, from about the age of two years onwards, by a mother substitute (as was the heroine of her second novel, Helen Huntingdon), who was the sister of her dead mother.[17] Her mother had not fallen ill until fourteen months after giving birth to Anne, so she and her baby daughter must have enjoyed some special time together, although Anne would not consciously have remembered it. After her death, Aunt Elizabeth Branwell, who came from the sunnier climes of Penzance, arrived to stay at the Parsonage, having accepted, one might say rather self-sacrificially, to give up her own comfortable existence to care instead for her dead sister's six children. Such a decision could not have been an easy one for her to make and illustrates how Anne's sense of Christian values in life was influenced, from a young age, by the very example of her virtual 'step-mother'. In order to manage, as best she could, this large family of five girls and one boy, Aunt Branwell sent away the four older girls in the spring of

1824, to be educated at Cowan Bridge School. Unfortunately, it was from this school (alias the infamous 'Lowood School' in *Jane Eyre*) that Maria and Elizabeth Brontë returned home ill, to die shortly afterwards, Maria on 6 May 1825 and Elizabeth on 15 June 1825. Consequently, for the next five and a half years, fearful of sending away to school the remaining four children, Aunt Branwell and their brilliant, dynamic but eccentric father educated them themselves at the Parsonage until Charlotte's departure for Roe Head School in January 1831, when Anne was about eleven years old. On Charlotte's return home from Roe Head in 1832, she virtually took over her father's role as teacher, so allowing him more free time as his eyesight worsened. Anne shared much of her childhood lessons, including Latin, with Branwell and witnessed, at first hand, the indulgence shown to him as the only son of the family, not only in the school-room but everywhere and all the time. She saw Branwell's many failures, including his unsuccessful attempt at gaining a place in the local grammar school and she was 'already developing the maturity to perceive the failure and to contemplate the underlying causes'.[18] It was to the disastrous consequences of this laxity towards boys and excessive sheltering of girls, which she observed in her own and others' homes, but mostly in her two posts as governess, that Anne was to react through the mouths of her fictional heroines, Agnes Grey and Helen Huntingdon. By drawing on her experience as a governess of caring for some very undisciplined and consequently unmanageable children and young adults, Anne reveals the harm to both sexes of such an education.

As already mentioned, when her eldest sister, Charlotte, took up a post as teacher at Roe Head School, Anne joined her there as a free pupil, some time before 27 October 1835, replacing her other sister, Emily, who had been unable to endure being so far away from her beloved home. This was Anne's first big separation from her loved ones and the loneliness and illness she experienced there during the two and a quarter years of her school education from the age of 15 years on made their mark upon her.[19] The school's somewhat Calvinistic approach to religion and the multitude of dissenting voices to her and her father's and aunt's point of view on salvation (which tended towards the more loving, Wesleyan approach, where all can be forgiven of their sins and accepted by Jesus Christ), might well have perturbed and shocked her. Later on, in her novels, Anne shows the disparity between the two religious views of Roe Head and of the Parsonage, reflected in Hatfield's ideas of God as a 'terrible taskmaster' and in Mr. Weston's thoughts on his Maker as being a 'benevolent Father'.

In any case, Anne most certainly suffered a spiritual crisis at school, which Winifred Gérin states was the result of her aunt's over-rigid upbringing. However, it seems far more likely that this crisis came about as a result of the absolute rigidity of Roe Head School. Anne, as a favourite of Aunt Branwell's and the youngest child of that large family, had always received a great deal of love and attention at home and had lived a comparatively free and easy life at the Parsonage, as Charlotte's friend, Ellen Nussey had remarked[20] and must have found it extremely hard to accept the Calvinist teaching at Roe Head School, which seemed to be that 'a person who was gloomy and melancholy must be a person from whom God has turned his face, one destined for the doom of reprobation.'[21] Such a harsh, unforgiving doctrine affected her health and filled her with dread and natural apprehension about which category she herself fitted into. As already intimated, she worried too about her brother, Branwell, who constantly expressed doubts over his salvation, stating, through his own poetic outpourings that, because of his shortcomings, he was evidently not one of the elect and was therefore doomed to go to Hell.

> 'Nay, all is lost. I cannot bear
> In mouldering dust to disappear,
> And Heaven will not the gloom dispel –
> Since were there one, my home were Hell –
> No Hope, no Hope, and oh farewell'.[22]

Yet, even before arriving at Roe Head, Brontë had begun to work out her own rejection of the Calvinist doctrine of eternal damnation for non-elect beings and had started to move towards the idea of a Heaven for everyone. Coming as she did from a somewhat law-abiding, if loving, background, where she had formed a strong relationship with her father and her substitute mother, her time in a school, in which she was starved of affection and where not even her sister Charlotte paid her much attention, seemed very harsh. *A Voice from the Dungeon,* written in October 1837, by Anne's Gondal persona Marina Sabina, reveals the depression from which Anne was suffering at the time of writing this poem, which indicates an overwhelming desire to retire from 'the bustling world above'. Anne describes 'a place of solitude and gloom' with 'No hope, no pleasure', where even dreams give no relief. However, one dream gives her some pleasure, in which Anne speaks of glimpsing her own baby boy and his father. Yet, her accursed scream wakes her and causes these visions to vanish, at which point her suffering begins again. She says: 'And I must live and die alone', a touch of déjà-vu, when one considers the early death of the only romantic figure in her life, William Weightman, and indeed, not that much later, of herself. Such dreams of marriage and parenthood were not to be for her. On 24 January 1838, Brontë writes in one of her Gondal poems, *The Captive's Dream*, of her inability to rise from her 'dark dungeon floor'. Again, on 26 January 1838, she speaks of her growing despair, saying that the wind 'is nothing to the gloomy silence/I have had to bear'. She cries out in her agony that 'hot tears' are better far 'than the dull gnawing tearless [time]/The stupor of despair.'[23]

At Roe Head, where it is more than likely she met with variants of her theories and severe opposition to her own not yet finalised thoughts, she became very ill, depressed and fearful on her return home for the Christmas holidays of 1837, as becomes evident from the account of the Rev. James La Trobe's visit to her at school in January 1838. Her request for a visit from a Moravian church minister from Mirfield could well have been to avoid being confronted, in her very weak state, by a Calvinist. In a text related by Mr. Scruton, James La Trobe reveals to us the content of his meeting with Anne during her illness at the school, and how after his visits she responded to his views that even the redeemed man was capable of sinning and feeling doubts and yet being forgiven anew. This apparently reassured her greatly for, in the state she was in, she was suffering tremendously from self-doubts as to whether or not she was indeed saved. Again, on 20 December 1841, she writes of her despondency in a poem of that name.[24] But by 28 May 1843, in her poem, *A Word to the Calvinists*, Anne had reached a conclusion in her faith and was ready to advocate her own particular doctrine, stressing her heartfelt desire that all would be saved through God's love, even without repentance of their past wicked life:

> 'That even the wicked shall at last
> Be fitted for the skies;
> And, when their dreadful doom is past,
> To light and life arise.'

This stanza emphasises her hope that as God loves all men, no-one would be allowed to perish. The poem also speaks of Purgatory which allows 'the dross' to be 'purged away'. This is an interesting departure from the orthodox, traditional Anglican viewpoint and figures as a question of paramount importance in her second novel,[25] where her heroine, Helen, just before her marriage to Arthur Huntingdon, scours her Bible for quotations to support such a theory. Through Helen, Anne voices her opinion that even such as her brother Branwell, who was convinced of his rejection by God, would still be admitted to His kingdom, after a time of purification in the redemptive fires of Purgatory:

'That when the cup of wrath is drained,
The metal purified,
They'll cling to what they once disdained,
And live by Him that died'.[26]

At last Anne's two and a quarter years of education came to an end, which, although provided by the well-meaning Wooler sisters, was still unfortunately deficient in love. As a result of it, she found herself sufficiently equipped academically to obtain subsequent posts as a governess. In those days there were no set qualifications needed and according to Lady Wilson: 'Governesses needed no diplomas only patience and to be genteel'.[27]

Influence of Visits

Visits of certain parishioners to the Parsonage of Haworth to her father, the Rev. Patrick Brontë provided Anne with valuable information for her novels. One particular visit, which might well have been reported to her by letter, when she was away at Thorp Green, took place in November 1840. It concerned a certain Mrs. Collins, 'wife of Busfeild's curate in Keighley, who had been on friendly terms with the Brontës', and whose tale was truly terrible. Mrs. Collins spoke: 'of her wretched husband's drunken, extravagant, profligate habits. She asked papa's advice; there was nothing she said but ruin before them. They owed debts which they could never pay. She expected Mr. C's instant dismissal from his curacy; she knew from bitter experience, that his vices were utterly hopeless. He treated her and her child savagely; with much more to the same effect. Papa advised her to leave him for ever, and go home, if she had a home to go to. She said this was what she had long resolved to do; and she would leave him directly, as soon as Mr. B dismissed him.'[28]

This is a theme easily recognisable in Anne's second novel. Apparently Mrs. Collins did not, however, follow Patrick Brontë's unconventional advice, for her husband was retained in his post for quite a while longer, where she stayed on with him – even bearing him another child. Yet, after this initial visit, she revisited the Parsonage once more, six and a half years later in April 1847, when Anne Brontë would have been at home and therefore able to hear from Mrs. Collins' own lips the sequel to her tale. Apparently, the Rev. John Collins had continued his vicious habits both in England and also in France and had abandoned his wife 'to disease and total destitution in Manchester'.[29] Mrs. Collins had managed to overcome the vile venereal disease to which she had succumbed and even to reinstate herself in society, by keeping a lodging house in a residential part of Manchester. Her arrival at the Parsonage must have caused quite a stir, and her story of 'undeserved sufferings, agonies and physical degradation' could only have provoked deep revolt and sympathy in Anne's breast. Indeed, Mrs. Collin's second visit to the Parsonage might well have taken place at just the right time for Anne to recall and use such a theme, and to encourage her in her already pronounced reflections on one of the ills of society, that of the lack of preparedness of young women to cope with such ordeals and the lack of escape offered them by the laws of the day. Undoubtedly, this dreadful account inspired Anne's *The Tenant of Wildfell Hall*, where Helen Huntingdon suffers from somewhat similar vicissitudes at the hands of her depraved husband, Arthur, fortunately without being contaminated by syphilis but nevertheless compelled to take eventual flight with her child from the family home, as Mrs. Collins had done.

Anne was also influenced by the visits to the Parsonage of two of her ex-pupils, Bessie and Mary Robinson. She corresponded regularly with them after leaving Thorp Green and their animated lives supplied her with much of the necessary news of the latest escapades of the gentry. Such information, she no doubt, incorporated in her *Tenant*.

Many other visits took place including those Anne made to the homes of her relatives and of Charlotte's friends, Ellen Nussey and Mary Taylor, where she had contrasted the luxury of their family set-ups with her own, using such observations as material for her later writings. She thought of Ellen as her own friend too, and in her last days requested by letter that Ellen accompany Charlotte and herself on that final journey to Scarborough just before her death in May 1849. At that point, Anne was relatively well-off and could easily afford to pay the expenses to Scarborough. Her aunt's legacy and the royalties from her two novels had entirely changed her financial situation, but too late.

At the beginning of her school summer holidays in 1836, desperate to return as soon as possible to the Parsonage after a long and unhappy term, Anne rather reluctantly accepted the invitation, along with Charlotte, to spend a week at the home of her godmother, Elizabeth Franks,[30] who lived relatively close to Roe Head School. This visit might well have been remembered by her later on with a degree of guilt at her lack of enthusiasm, for shortly after this event, Elizabeth Franks died rather suddenly while visiting Anne's other godmother, Fanny Outhwaite, in Bradford. While staying at the Franks, Anne was invited to accompany Charlotte to Lascelles Hall, where Charlotte's ex school fellow, Amelia Walker, lived. Dr. Chitham describes this visit as Anne's first experience of 'the kind of society where she would eventually serve as governess and discuss in her novels.'

Influence of Personal Experience

Another source of her inspiration on bringing up children came from her personal experience as a Sunday School teacher in Haworth National Sunday School, which opened its doors in June 1832, when Anne was twelve years of age. Teaching the children to read the Bible was one of the main aims of instruction, so, as one of the volunteers who ran it, Anne would have increased her knowledge of the Scriptures by teaching the young folk there.

However, her greatest inspiration as regards child-rearing undoubtedly came from her personal experience as a governess. Anne worked with two sets of employers and observed at first hand what took place in their households. Initially, she worked for the Inghams at Blake Hall from 8 April 1839 for a year, and then for the Robinsons at Thorp Green from spring 1841 to July 1845.

Such situations were amongst the few acceptable openings available to middle-class, unmarried ladies like herself, who were well-educated but relatively poor. In fact, women had very few other options open to them at the time except to become a lady's companion, a governess or, if prepared to incur the displeasure of society, using their own names as female writers. Yet, even the courageous Brontë sisters first wrote under the pseudonyms of Currer, Ellis and Acton Bell to avoid detection. Not that many years after their deaths, in 1865, Charlotte Mary Yonge, using her own name, wrote the novel, *The Clever Woman of the Family,* in which she attempted to highlight the difficulties of women in finding either a marital partner or employment because of the surplus of women over men. Yonge's novel is in part a response to the Surplus Women Question. This whole question had come to light in the Census of 1851 and had led to many discussions on the subject of the pressing need for society to recognise the necessity for more openings for unmarried, educated women than the few avenues allowed them. The statistics revealed by the 1851 Census counted six million adult women in all, i.e. 500,000 more women than men, three million of whom had to work to maintain themselves, and of which there were two million unmarried. The need for women to support themselves was more than evident, but unfortunately the possibilities of work were very limited to 'three, or most four, limited occupations, to wit teaching, needlework, domestic service, and novel-writing'.[31] Harriet Martineau speaks of 'spirit-broken governesses and starving needlewomen,'[32] very likely based on what Charlotte told her on her visit to her home in the Lake District.

Undoubtedly, being a governess was not an easy job, for she had the unenviable task of bringing up other people's children without enjoying any power over them to exercise control. Once installed in her employers' home, the governess often experienced great loneliness, as she was recognised neither as the equal of her employers nor of the servants. This aspect of a governess's life is highlighted in an article by James R. Simmons, Jr. on autobiographies written by real-life governesses of the Victorian era. He concludes that most of their difficulties came from class distinction, where being 'equalled with a servant at best or a nobody at worst' cannot have been immensely pleasant.[33]

On 8 April 1839, when Anne took up her first post as governess to the two eldest children of the Inghams of Blake Hall – a boy of six and a girl of five years – she was doubtless not as knowledgeable as she later became 'of the many Governess debates of the 1840s' to which she contributed greatly 'by writing in both her novels of the power struggles encountered by the educated, middle-class woman forced to take on paid work and consequently subjected to a lack of respect from both her employers and society at large'.[34] More work on this topic has emerged in Bettina L. Knapp's recently published article where she attempts to show Anne as intent on instructing the public through the narrative of the novel of the 'plight and working conditions of the unmarried girls and women who are obliged to go out into the world and earn a living'.[35] Knapp sees Anne as preaching women's education as the first step towards economic independence and self-respect and using her novel to change society's negative views accordingly. This relatively valid view is seemingly based on Mary Wollstonecroft's more politically inclined brand of feminism, whereas Anne's own desire for independence was only for such as she could accept within the confines outlined by her religious convictions and certainly not that which would compete in any way with man's authority.

The Victorian idea that homelife was a domestic heaven was most certainly exposed as fallacious in Anne's second novel as being, in certain circumstances, a domestic hell. She reveals how a bad relationship between husband and wife could jeopardise any possible marriage bliss and most certainly ruin the upbringing of children. Anne blames this unhappiness on women's limited education, and their consequent inability to make a reasoned choice. A lack of parental guidance also meant that their education was only sufficient to afford them a limited choice of employment if they were unable to marry.

In her two posts, Anne became increasingly aware of the unhappiness of her employers' marriage situations and of their lack of care or discipline towards their children. She noted how they ruined their sons by not restraining them from committing any evil and reared their daughters in ignorance, merely to become decorative future possessions of rich, eligible bachelors. Within the household of her second employers, the Robinsons, whose daughters Anne tutored and whose son was later to be tutored by her brother, Branwell, she witnessed a hedonistic life-style and many other things which truly upset her.[36] Indeed, in the back of her prayer book, she wrote, during her stay there, 'Sick of mankind and their disgusting ways'. Branwell, having been engaged as tutor, through Anne's instigation, unfortunately fell under his employer's spell. According to contemporary accounts,[37] Mrs. Robinson seduced him soon after he was employed by her husband and herself, only for this illicit liaison to be discovered in the summer of 1845 by the former, at which moment in time Branwell was instantly dismissed from his post. As mentioned it is reported as being through the witness of the Robinson's gardener that Mr. Robinson was informed of the affair between Branwell and his wife. This garden involvement is reproduced in *The Tenant of Wildfell Hall,* where Helen gets to know of her husband's adultery – a touch of role reversal – by witnessing her husband's behaviour with Annabella Wilmot/Lowborough in the shrubbery of her gardens. After Branwell's dismissal and especially after Mrs. Robinson's re-marriage, he set out on the road to drug dependence and alcoholism, so introducing his family to three years of misery, which ended with his death in September 1848. Indeed, up to mid-1848, Branwell was apparently still receiving funds from that source to help keep him quiet and feed his habits. Anne's guilt at having introduced her brother to this corrupt household, in her attempt to help him find a suitable post, caused her to draw on her experience of these painful years, from July 1845 onwards, and use it as the basis of her inspiration for *The Tenant of Wildfell Hall* and of her indictment of the parental education of her day.

In this second novel, written from early 1847 onwards and published on 7 July 1848, Anne uses as its main themes what she herself has actually read about or witnessed in the homes of gentry during her short working life – adultery, drug addiction and excessive use of alcohol – in order to illustrate how the so-called gentleman, Arthur Huntingdon, Helen's husband, who is adept at all three of the sins listed, proves too much of a challenge for the redemptive claims of his wife, just as, no doubt, Branwell, who also partook of all three and died at 31 years of age of Delirium Tremens, proved an over-heavy burden for Rev. Patrick Brontë and his three remaining daughters. Eventually, Helen has to admit to herself her failure to reform her rake of a husband, recognizing at last that such a transformation could only come from God. Yet, fulfilling the deeply Evangelical intent of the novel, Helen still doggedly persists in her aim to convert Arthur to Christianity before his death.

Anne certainly did not consider herself competent to reform single-handed the errors and abuses of society but felt it her duty to tell the truth about them and so contribute 'her humble quota towards so good an aim.' She was evidently not writing just for amusement and was bravely prepared to 'speak an unpalatable truth' if necessary.[38] She, in no way, sets herself up as an expert on marital advice, nor does she lay down a fixed set of rules on parenting. Instead, she relates her thoughts in an honest and unbiased way, giving examples of the difficulties encountered by her fictitious personae in their respective relationships to illustrate how such situations could be better dealt with. Through her clever use of dialogue, she presents each example from two different angles, that of her heroine and that of the person or persons with whom she is dealing, so that the reader can make a personal judgment as to what truth Anne is trying to reveal in each of the scenes she chooses to depict. Psychologically aware for her times, she does not often intervene directly in her tale in order to force the reader to act in a particular way if presented with similar circumstances. Instead, she sets down the details of each scene with restraint, confining herself to realistic and rarely over-dramatic vocabulary to describe any occurrences. Her style is not at all prescriptive. Rather, she attempts to aid the reader by means of deduction rather than instruction, to become aware of any deficiencies in his own upbringing which could hinder his relationship and parenting skills. In this indirect way, via the scenes portrayed in her two novels, Anne provides the readers with a convincing argument for basing all parental and marital relationships on a firm set of biblical precepts, seeing all indifference to such values as the main reason for their failure. Such failures as are described in *Agnes Grey* and *The Tenant of Wildfell Hall* are mirrored in our present age, where more than three in ten marriages end in divorce and where people frequently turn away from long-standing relationships and the idea that marriage is sacred to 'the 'transient' pleasures of alcohol, drugs and recreational sex rather than to God'[39] Yet, nowadays, we cannot claim, as Anne could, inequality of the sexes in education and legal rights as an excuse for the multitude of broken marriages and cases of bad parenting which abound in modern times.

Anne's two novels, published when Branwell was living at home in the Parsonage depict her thoughts, anxieties and indeed her aims. She does not write just for her own solace but to help others escape the fate that had befallen her brother, and, from a religious point of view, also that of her sister, Emily. Much of Anne's experience had been confined to the landed gentry and upper-middle-class folk, yet, at the Parsonage, she had also come into contact with a whole cross-section of humanity and had heard the stories of many poor people, which might well have taught her to empathise with their situations. Consequently, her appealing message on parenting, although strongly orientated towards the educated classes, is also applicable to parents of any class or social status, for what she advocates is based on sound, rather than transient, values belonging to rich and poor alike.

Chapter Five:

Literary Influences

Yet another source of inspiration came from the books, magazines, monthly journals and newspapers which Anne Brontë read. Contrary to Charlotte's views, Anne, who was not thought of as 'learned' by her sister, who felt she did not 'fill her pitcher at the well-spring of others' minds',[40] did read widely. One has only to read her poetry to see the influence of writers such as William Cowper, George Herbert, William Wordsworth, Thomas Moore, Charles Wesley and even occasionally of Emily's favourite poets, Byron and Shelley. Dr. Juliet Barker gives a useful account in *The Brontës* of the books available in the Parsonage and also of those in the libraries to which Anne had access. These include, from 1833 on, Keighley Mechanics Institute, Ponden Hall, belonging to the Heaton family, where it seems the collection was dominated by eighteenth-century works with some French literature, Blake Hall Library from 1839-1840, and Thorp Green, from 1840-1845, which apparently had only one novel, Hannah More's *Coelebs in Search of a Wife,* the well-known conduct book giving guidance for females. Prior to seeing this book by More, Anne would have had access at the Parsonage to a copy of More's *Moral Sketches of prevailing opinions and manners,* which was undoubtedly required reading of the times, especially for literary households dominated by females as was the Brontës'. Anne also purchased her own copy of this book in 1843 to take back with her to Thorp Green, most probably to assist her in convincing her young lady charges to change their ways. Other books which inspired her seem to be John Bunyans's *Pilgrim's Progress,* Thomas à Kempis's *Of the Imitation of Christ,* Walter Scott's historical, Romantic tales, Isaac Watt's *Doctrine of the Passions*; John Milton's *Paradise Lost,* moral tales such as Samuel Johnson's *Rasselas,* Oliver Goldsmith's *The Vicar of Wakefield* and above all, *The Bible* and Anne's *Common Prayer Book,* both gifts from her godmothers.

The Bible and Common Prayer Book exerted, along with *Of the Imitation of Christ,* the greatest influence on the sentiment behind Anne Brontë's Writings:

'my word that goes out from my mouth:
It will not return to me empty,
But will accomplish what I desire
And achieve the purpose for which I sent it.'

The above quotation from Isaiah 55 verse 11, reflects her thoughts and reveals the attitude with which she wrote her two novels. Indeed, most of her warnings to parents in both her *Agnes Grey* and *The Tenant* are based on Proverbs 19 v.18:

'Discipline your son, for in that there is hope;
Do not be a willing party to his death'.

on Proverbs 13 v 24:

'He who spares the rod hates his son, but he who
loves him is careful to discipline him'.

on Proverbs 23 v 13:

'Do not withhold discipline from a child;
if you punish him with the rod, he will not die.
Punish him with the rod and save him from death'.

and especially on Proverbs 22 v.6:

'Train a child in the way he should go,
and when he is old (grown) he will not turn from it'.

Anne reveals her awareness of the dangers of Hell and Damnation, for which influence upon her her aunt is often blamed. It is probable that Anne, only outwardly timid and gentle, was profoundly strengthened by her aunt's and father's devotion to God, and found great solace in their daily readings from the Bible, feeling encouraged by the various biblical captions which abounded in the Parsonage. She daily witnessed the words on her aunt's teapot: 'to me to live is Christ, to die is gain'. On her own sampler, dated 23 January 1830, she sewed a strong message of correction based on Proverbs 3 vv.9-18, more particularly on verses 11-12, which was tempered by the statement that the Lord loved and delighted in his children and that his correction was a sign of his love:

'For whom the Lord loveth he correcteth,
Even as a father the son in whom he delighteth.
Happy is the man that findeth wisdom,
And the man that getteth understanding.'

Anne was guided from infancy by her aunt's strong Wesleyan Methodist principles. Aunt Branwell was truly opposed to the Calvinists and the Whitfield camp's belief in predestination with their claim that God determines man's fate before he is born, and denies the existence of Free Will on man's part. Instead, she taught her young charges that God was a God of love, who wanted to save all mankind, whilst still upholding her conviction that eternal punishment existed for the wicked who rejected God and disobeyed his commandments. Her strictness gave boundaries to her young charges, which, instead of causing them unhappiness by curtailing their freedom, was meant to allow them to act within safe limits. This evidently did not work with Branwell.

Anne's idea of what was expected of a young girl at that time would probably have been similar to the description given by her Uncle John Fennell, when he talked of the death 'in the full triumph of faith' of a young girl of nineteen years, Susanna Taylor of Penzance: 'grave and serious – no lightness or trifling – no foolish or vain conversation'.[41] Anne herself seems to have modelled not only her own behaviour but that of her fictional heroes and heroines on such a pattern. In her poem, *Vanitas Vanitatis* (4 September 1845), Anne gives a description of what man's way of life should be, which, more or less, gives an accurate portrayal of her own. He should:

> 'Assist his friends, forgive his foes
> Trust God, and keep His statutes still
> Upright and firm through good and ill –
> Thankful for all that God has given,
> Fixing his firmest hopes on Heaven;
> Knowing that earthly joys decay,
> But hoping through the darkest day'.

Edward Chitham rightly feels this poem is based on Ecclesiastes. It reads like the last chapter of that book, where Solomon, who has every worldly advantage, sees through all of this and urges man to trust and put his hope in God alone. It also expresses much of the hopefulness of the Psalms.

When Anne began a study of the Bible in 1841, she had already started to come to some conclusions on her faith. She listed but did not annotate chapters and verses of the Bible[42] marking, however, many passages including the Psalms. One of the Psalms which caught her attention was Psalm 145 vv.8-9, which shows that her overriding concern was to find examples of God's mercy and compassion for sinners. This was contrary to the accepted norm for Anglicanism of the day of there being eternal punishment in Hell for the wicked. Her Bible study seems aimed at finding a selection of biblical references to substantiate the doctrine she was busily formulating on Universal Salvation:

'The Lord is gracious and compassionate,
slow to anger and rich in love.
The Lord is good to all;
he has compassion on all he has made.'

Another verse, which also influenced her,

'I will refine them like silver
and test them like gold.
They will call on my name
and I will answer them;
I will say, "They are my people",
and they will say, "The Lord is our God".'

comes from one of the minor prophets, Zechariah 13: v.9, and fully supports her idea of salvation for all, after a period of refinement by fire. This is reflected in her poem, *A Word to the Calvinists,* which she wrote on 28 May 1843, where she talks of 'dross' being 'purged away' and 'the metal purified' before they can 'cling to what they once disdained/And live by him that died'.

Many other references to the Bible, too numerous to recount here, can be found in her novels, including Helen's many quotations of verses to her aunt prior to her marriage with Huntingdon, through which she supports her theory of Salvation for the whole of mankind, sinners and all. In *Agnes Grey,* Mr. Grey's attitude to money seems to have been taken from 1 Timothy 6: v.9: 'People who want to get rich fall into temptation and a trap and into many foolish and harmful desires that plunge men into ruin and destruction'. Mr. Grey did get entrapped by his desire to provide his wife with greater wealth. This did indeed bring about his downfall and his death. Another example is that of Anne's Rosalie Murray who marries entirely for money and, as a result, falls into misery.

Another verse which evidently supported Anne throughout the drudgery and occasionally malicious circumstances she experienced in her employment as a governess to the Inghams and especially to the Robinsons' could well have been Luke 6 verses 27-28:

'But I tell you who hear me: Love your enemies,
do good to those who hate you,
bless those who curse you,
pray for those who ill-treat you.'

We can certainly see how such sentiment helped her portrayal of
how Agnes handles Rosalie's spitefulness when she is trying, simply
out of boredom, to win over Mr. Weston's affections away from Agnes.
Agnes is compelled to suffer all in silence and even to have to remain
cheerful under such circumstances.

In addition to the *Bible*, Anne might well have spent a great deal of
time reading Thomas À Kempis's *Of the Imitation of Christ,* whose
four booklets entitled *Admonitions 'useful for a spiritual life;
concerning inward things; of internal consolation; and concerning the
Communion',* are based on the Scriptures. Practically all the advice
contained in these booklets seems relevant to the way in which Anne
thought and conducted herself, and, more importantly here, wrote her
novels. The titles of the chapters on *Of thinking humbly of Ourselves
(I: ii); Of the inward life (II: I); That the Longings and Desires of our
Hearts are to be examined and moderated (III: XI); That a man should
not be too much dejected, even when he falleth into some defects (III:
LVII);* and particularly *Of thoroughly searching our own conscience,
and of holy purposes of amendment (IV: VII),*[43] speak for themselves.
Two particular examples are worth considering: the first from *III: XI*
on the moderation of our desires, which, combined with Anne's
reading of 1 Corinthians 9, must have influenced her greatly in her
description in *The Tenant,* where her heroine struggles to overcome
her desires to seek revenge and where Lord Lowborough's battles to
moderate his violent feelings over his wife's adultery with
Huntingdon and to refuse the request by Mr. Hattersley and Mr.
Grimsby to fight a duel. Helen supports Lowborough in his attempts
to leave vengeance to God, although, to her husband's friends, his
refusal reduces him to 'an object of scorn' (p.352). These friends seem
incapable of understanding Lowborough's valiant struggles to stay
true to his beliefs and thereby overcome his desire to fight or kill his
former friend for deceiving him in this way.

The second example comes from the fourth booklet *(IV: VII),* which
concerns self-examination. As mentioned in the Introduction, Anne
examines herself throughout her writings in her search to know
herself better and offer herself answers to her questions. It is very
likely that she was influenced in this by John Locke, whose premise
that knowledge is arrived at by questioning one's own experience and
memory was well known. Anne's tormenting self-questioning on the
subject of Calvinism in Roe Head School at the time of her illness
must have been greatly assuaged by her reading of Thomas À Kempis,
especially by those of his verses which talk of the forgiveness of sins.
Her poems reveal her constant anxiety at straying from the straight
and narrow path, a fear which was doubtless calmed by the visit of the
Moravian priest, La Trobe, with his message of a God of love who

truly pardons all sinners. His visit and her reading might well have helped to clarify her mind on the question of Universal Salvation, upon which issue she was deliberating even at that young age. A verse offering her comfort here is based on Ezekiel, XVIII (22, 23): 'And when a man shall have done what lieth in him, and shall be truly penitent, how often soever he shall come to me for pardon and grace, "As I live," saith the Lord, "who will not the death of a sinner, but rather that he be converted and live, I will not remember his sins any more, but they shall all be forgiven him."'

Influence of Hannah More
Anne's strongly held religious views were also undoubtedly influenced by edifying authors such as Hannah More and Mary Brunton, who wrote quite blatantly as Evangelicals, but set out very much as Anne did to instruct at the same time as entertain 'a public hungry for fiction as well as for moral guidance'.[44] Indeed, Anne's similar insistence that art instructs and entertains at the same time as providing a moral focus, finds its fulfilment in her use of the novel as an art form to promote her aim to educate the 'young and thoughtless traveller' and give him or her an awareness of 'the snares and pitfalls of life' rather than 'to cover them with branches and flowers.' Her words are startlingly similar to those used by More in her *Coelebs in search of a wife (1808),* where More states that the purpose of a writer's knowledge is to mend the world and that 'A writer employs this knowledge honestly, when he points out the snares and pitfalls of vice. But when he covers those snares and pitfalls with flowers' he cannot commit 'a deeper injury to society' (*Coelebs,* p.133).

More, a well-known English Romantic author (1745-1833) wrote her *Coelebs,* with its emphasis on parenting, education, marriage, and religion, to help society reform and conduct its life within the confines of faith She wrote in a heavily didactic style very different from Brontë's restrained, more natural approach. Both authors use the name of their hero/heroine as the title of their novels, but Brontë's *Agnes Grey* is certainly not as pretentious a title as *Coelebs* meaning a bachelor, which is a name that More's hero renounces (addressed throughout the novel as Charles), once he has found and married his ideal woman.

As already mentioned, this, the only novel that More ever wrote, was the sole novel in the library of Thorp Green, where Anne Brontë worked, so it is highly likely that she knew it intimately and took on board the contents of this conduct book, which greatly resembles *Agnes Grey*, for both novels are intent on giving good advice on the manners and social duties of the times in order to effect a behavioural

change in society. In *Coelebs*, we meet Charles, a bachelor, in search of
his ideal match, a wife,who will submit to her husband and 'study
household good' and yet show evidence of 'intellectual worth'.[45] He
has been well advised by his mother before her death, as to what
qualities to seek in a woman, who, according to her, should be: 'a
friend, a companion, and a wife'. Indeed, his mother voices More's
own opinion as to how a woman should be educated, which is reflected
in Anne Brontë's ideas on the subject. More says: 'I call education, not
that which is made up of the shreds and patches of useless arts, but
that which inculcates principles, polishes taste, regulates temper,
cultivates reason, subdues the passions, directs the feelings,
habituates to reflection, trains to self-denial, and, more especially,
that which refers all actions, feelings, sentiments, tastes, and passions
to the love and fear of God.' (*Coelebs*, p.13). In giving this definition
Charles' mother is describing the way she would wish her son's future
wife to be educated, for she feels strongly that the education of the day
is not conducive to domestic happiness. Brontë reflects these ideas on
education very comprehensively in her novels, thereby revealing
indirectly why she needed to purchase a copy of one of More's books to
use in her teaching of the two young Robinson girls on her return to
them after the Christmas holidays in 1843. Her hope might well have
been that by directing their reading towards such a 'good' book
something of it would have rubbed off on them too. Not for More, nor
for Brontë, was the radical approach to women's rights of Mary
Wollstonecraft. Both were far more concerned, as strong Christians,
in supporting social stability and promoting the biblical, rather than
the political, truths of life. This does not mean to say that Brontë was
unaware of the double standards of her day, the hypocrisy of her
times, or that she does not oppose such injustice whole-heartedly. It is
more to suggest that what she offers her readers is her own experience
as a young single lady, a paid employee of the gentry, who has
witnessed the unfairness of the class structure and attitude in
existence in her age. She seems to have quietly resolved, very like
More, to help the public to come to a better understanding, from the
Christian point of view, of what educational practices ought to be
adopted to allow society to change for the better and for women to be
trained to find independence intellectually, yet still retain their
'conjugal obedience' (*Coelebs*, p.10).

   Brontë's novel flows more readily than More's and its message,
although strongly Evangelistic, by not being presented in the same
didactic way, is far more easily absorbed by the reader. This is because
of Brontë's use of amusing illustrations of day-to-day experiences
narrated by Agnes in the first person, which give a reality and a
personal quality to her account. In *Coelebs*, we listen to Charles, who

also narrates in the first person, but who is far too frequently interrupted by various conversations on different topics in the course of the story-line, incorporating both monologues and dialogues. This allows a certain unreality to enter the novel through the constant third person interventions of the authorial voice. This exposition of More's own views, which occurs a little too often not to hinder the flow of the tale, causes quite a large degree of jerkiness to the novel. *Coelebs* discusses and gives far more guide-lines on a greater variety of subjects than does *Agnes Grey*. Yet, even so, More's and Brontë's main warnings, given in their respective novels, are very similar and relate mainly to religion, marriage and the bringing up of children, which issues are all three interwoven. Through More's descriptions of what goes on in many different households, we are introduced in *Coelebs* to her ideal parents, the Stanleys, who, from the basis of their happy marriage, rear their children by strict adherence to Christian tenets. More's interest in this subject of parenting is reflected by Brontë in *Agnes Grey* and also in *The Tenant*, where we witness Brontë's attempts to warn her public against the effects on children and on young men and women of any teaching, which does not adhere to a moral code of ethics.

More's novel begins by emphasising the importance of a child's formation from birth through infancy to adulthood. Charles' parents are depicted (as are Agnes's), as a caring and loving couple whose main aim is to train their child to grow up strong in his faith and in good works. After the death of his father, Charles is seen lovingly to carry out his duty to look after his mother until she too dies: 'there is no affection of the human heart more exquisitely pure than that which is felt by a grateful son towards a mother who fostered his infancy with kindness, watched over his childhood with anxiety, and his youth with an interest compounded of all that is tender, wise, and pious' (*Coelebs,* p.14). Brontë recalls such sentiments in Agnes's own attitude to her mother and her dying father, in Edward Weston's account of his dead parents, and also in Gilbert Markham's respectful attitude to his mother. Charles, after arranging all his affairs, eventually leaves his home at the Priory, obeying his parents' wish that he should travel to visit various friends of theirs in order to find a wife. However, they had advised him strongly not to make a decision as to whom to marry until he has first visited the Stanley household. His father describes the state of marriage as a 'union between intellectual and well-bred persons', where the woman needs to be informed, have an elegant mind and be virtuous and pious (*Coelebs,* p.15). En route to his first visit in London, Charles soliloquizes on the attributes he is seeking in his future wife who must be 'elegant', 'sensible', 'prudent' and 'well-informed, or she could not educate [his]

children', 'well-bred', 'consistent' and 'pious' (p.16). During this first
visit, he witnesses a wife who is a poor manager at table, reminding
Brontë's readers of Mr. Bloomfield's great tirade against his wife
when he chides her on her poor domestic management, but then
surreptitiously eats in silence some small choice bits of the meat he
has despised as being so badly cooked. Brontë's dry humour in this
latter illustration allows the image of Mr. Bloomfield's bad temper
and gluttony to be recollected very readily, whereas More's example,
which she treats far more seriously and with over-much of a
moralistic tone, is not as memorable owing to its lack of humour. The
parenting involvement in both cases, however, is emphasised, for
Charles notes that the woman in question has made her daughters
'learn everything' without helping them to distinguish the subjects on
which to concentrate, such as domestic management of a household.

A further parenting tip, which Brontë evidently absorbs from her
reading of More, is provided by Charles' next visit to Sir John and
Lady Belfield of Cavendish Square, where everything passes off in
wonderful fashion until after dinner, when Charles, awaiting an
interesting conversation, finds that the whole proceedings are
violently interrupted by the rushed entry of half a dozen children
'pretty barbarians' who, through their antics, totally stop all possible
attempts at serious conversation. The six-year-old son is seen to act as
naughtily as young Tom Bloomfield in *Agnes Grey*, for he tries to upset
his sister's glass at table but instead overthrows his own, brimful with
port wine, onto the white dress of one of the young ladies. For this, he
is not subjected to any other punishment than to be dismissed from
the dining-room. This is reminiscent of the scene where Brontë
stresses the over-indulgence shown to the Bloomfield children and
emphasises the bad effects of drink on a child, as she shows us in the
example in *The Tenant* of young Arthur, a child very similar in age to
this six-year-old boy, who is plied with liquor by his father.

After meeting up with Mr. and Mrs. Ranby at Hampstead and their
three rather scantily and immodestly dressed daughters, who offend
Charles because of his mother's maxim for 'consistency' by their show
against purity and modesty, Charles decides that what he needs is a
woman informed enough to 'contribute her full share towards
spending a wet winter cheerfully in the country' (p.25). This is again
what one could imagine to be the thoughts of Edward Weston or of
Gilbert Markham, as regards their future wife. Charles blames the
Ranby daughters' education rather than their disposition (as does
Agnes Grey when speaking of Rosalie Murray), and he decides that
the three greatest inducements in the choice of a wife are 'that a man
may have a directress for his family, a preceptress for his children, and
a companion for himself'. Once again this resembles what Edward

Weston achieves in Agnes, who is the companion that he states he lacked and, from Agnes's sparse comments at the end of *Agnes Grey*, we see how well she is managing her household and how she is also educating her three children herself.

More parenting advice is offered by More as regards the Belfields – note the similar name to the Bloomfields, used by Brontë in her *Agnes Grey* – where Lady Belfield encourages no vice in her children but does not 'sufficiently check those indications which are the seeds of vice' (*Coelebs*, p.34). She does at least reprove them but never tries to implant in them a principle to stop the evil in its tracks 'so that the individual error and the individual correction were constantly recurring'. We meet this too in *Agnes Grey*, where Mrs. Bloomfield, who attributes great saintliness to her children, never fully checks their faults and even refuses to admit them when they are blatantly carried out in front of her. An example is when Tom refuses to tidy up his room for both Agnes and his mother, who then grants him the forbidden tea, although he has not complied with her request. More tells us that 'infant prevarication unnoticed, and unchecked, is the prolific seed of subterfuge, of expediency, of deceit, of falsehood, of hypocrisy' (*Coelebs*, p.158), a thought which Brontë certainly reflects in her first novel, where Agnes points out the need to check the Bloomfield children before they grow any older or it will be too late. When Mrs. Bloomfield notices some faults in her little daughter, she prefers to blame Agnes for them rather than herself or the children, for, like Lady Belfield, she feels that education is the cure for all evils for her children who are 'innocent little things'. Lady Belfield's ideas on education contrast sharply with those of Mrs. Ranby, who feels that education is worthless and can achieve nothing, but resemble those of Brontë's Mrs. Bloomfield, In Mrs. Bloomfield's case, there is the added proviso that no effort is to be expended by her children.

The only governess we meet in *Coelebs* is Fanny Stokes, who is, at the time of our meeting her, a poor flower-maker, but who has not always been so. She, like Agnes Grey, has received an excellent education which has encouraged her in 'her understanding and principles' which are 'equally good' (p.53). Unlike Agnes, she is depicted as extremely beautiful which 'made good people afraid to take her into the house, and exposed her to danger from those of the opposite description' (p.53). This is more reminiscent of Mary Brunton's Ellen Percy in *Discipline*, who, when she becomes a governess, suffers because of her beauty. This does not apply to Agnes, who is plain and ordinary and the first governess to be portrayed as such in fiction.

When Charles finally arrives at Stanley Grove to visit Mr. and Mrs. Stanley and their children, he meets Lucilla, their eldest daughter, to whom he is very much attracted. He struggles not to abandon himself to the passion of his love, relying instead on his religion which, although it does not extinguish his passions, has taught him to regulate them. The way in which the Stanley children are brought up differs widely from that of the Belfields, for they are raised in 'Habitual industry, quiet exertion, successive employments, affectionate intercourse, and gay and animated relaxation' to make up 'the round of their cheerful day' (p.66). This successful programme is advocated to combat what Mr. Stanley calls the education in vogue or 'Mahometan education', which consists of educating a woman simply to attract a man in marriage. Mary Brunton also reproaches this kind of education through her character, Julia Arnold, who is 'educated to marry', and Brontë is evidently influenced by such ideas as we see in her Rosalie Murray, who is also educated only to please and get her man, completely against Agnes's advice and instructions. Brontë also follows More's and Wollstonecraft's views on not allowing girls to read too many novels, which make them ready to submit to passion but do not inform them 'of the miseries attendant on an indiscreet attachment' (p.82), as we see from Rosalie Murray, who spends many hours reading or pretending to read novels, in the fields of her estate, and whose attachment certainly does lead to wretchedness.

More speaks on the question of over-indulgence, as does Brontë, and shows us through her characters, such as Lady Belfield, the error of an 'excess of kindness and candour', which leads to over-indulgence of her children and an over-favourable construction of their errors. Agnes herself describes how she, as a child, had been treated excessively kindly by her parents, which had certainly not helped her self-assurance when she left the family home. Although sincerely devout, Lady Belfield is reluctant at first to be secluded from the world, and is contrasted with Lady Aston, also sincerely devout but over-melancholy, who prefers total seclusion from the world for herself and her daughters. More then provides the best and most balanced model in the Stanleys, which helps both the Belfields and Astons to make 'their virtues more active' (p.76) and more enjoyable. Lucilla has been well trained by her parents, especially by their joint efforts, for the father has 'diffused his own spirit through the whole family', especially 'his candour, his humility, his constant reference, not as a topic of discourse, but as a principle of conduct, to the Gospel' (p.106). These are principles followed by Brontë's heroines. Indeed the Belfields learn a great deal from the Stanleys, becoming more conscious of their injudicious use of indulgence and little control over their children. Mrs. Stanley speaks at length on 'the new school of philosophy and politics' which increases 'insubordination of children' (p.127). She feels strongly that children should not be allowed to dictate, a sentiment shared by Jane Austen, who, in her *Sense and Sensibility,* shows us Lady Middleton's children tyranizing the whole household, and in her *Persuasion,* Mary Elliot/Musgrove is seen to feel no love nor interest in her children, whom she indulges by allowing to run wild, simply to keep them away from herself. These women with no love of their children figure much in the fiction of the eighteenth-century and even later in Brontë's period, as her example of Annabella Wilmot shows us: for, conditioned as they are, to the detriment of their minds, to consider nothing of importance other than their own person, they find it nearly impossible to express love or carry out their maternal duties. More's attitude to such an education emerges by comparison and contrast, as does Brontë's in both novels, where Agnes is contrasted with Rosalie, and Helen with Annabella Wilmot. More shows how young ladies like Miss Amelia Rattle learn all subjects simply to rival their friends and give them all up as soon as they find their man. Rosalie admits a similar sentiment when she states that she would love to remain single and then capture the heart of someone desired by all the other young ladies. This reproach of the attitude to rivalry and conquest is common to both More and Brontë. The former is very much against learning just 'shreds and patches of education' taken on by girls for the wrong motives and without 'one ray of common sense, and one shade of delicacy'. Miss Rattle is used as a foil to the excellent Lucilla and again More states that she 'is rather the victim of a wretched education than of her own bad propensities' – a statement made often by Brontë as, for example, when Helen Huntingdon tries to explain to herself why her husband has turned out so badly.

Much parenting advice abounds in More, especially as both Charles and Lucilla pursue the qualities which they have seen exemplified by their fathers and practised by their mothers (p.112). It might also be worth noting how much emphasis More places on parents being of one mind in their dealings with their children. In a remark which Sir John Belfield makes to Mr. Stanley, we capture the efficacy of this union: 'Nothing impedes domestic regulations so effectually as where parents, from difference of sentiment, ill-humour or bad judgment, obstruct each other's plans, or where one parent makes the other insignificant in the eyes of their children' (p.124). Once again, Brontë takes up this idea of More's in both her novels, revealing how destructive the habit is. Initially, in *Agnes Grey* we see Mr. Bloomfield attack his wife's domestic management in front of the governess with no regard for the feelings of his wife, and, in *The Tenant,* Arthur deliberately tries, on many occasions, to hurt and make a fool of his wife in front of little Arthur, in order to undermine her domestic and parental authority. He even brings in a governess/mistress to 'educate' the child.

No financial incentives are ever advocated by More as bait for good behaviour, and the reward given to little Kate Stanley for performing best in the school-room is one of honour, for she is allowed to make and give to her mother a nosegay of flowers which she has helped to grow. When Agnes Grey succeeds in getting her charges to perform tolerably well in the school-room, she too resorts to similar measures to those advocated by More, a cheerful hymn for the good one and a dismal dirge to be recited by the naughty pupil. In More we see a comparison made between the boredom and destructive weariness, caused by giving too many expensive toys to children in the totally indulged Reynolds family, and the simplicity of the pleasures offered the Stanley children. It is evident that the Reynolds follow Rousseau's free and wild approach to education, allowing their children to take over their drawing room and whole house, whilst the stricter regime of the Stanleys gives happy contentment to their children with 'their cheap, yet lively pleasures . . . their successive occupations, their books, their animating exercise, their charitable rounds, their ardent friendships, the social table, at which the elder ones are companions, not rulers; the ever-varying pleasures of their garden' (p.128). We also see such ideas pursued both in Austen and Brontë, whose Agnes does her best to introduce to her charges a love of study, of charitable occupations and of good solid Christian principles.

Brontë was also influenced by More's thoughts on marriages of convenience'. Charles, certainly comments on 'the frequent indifference of parents to the moral, and especially to the religious character of the man who proposed himself' (p.130). More condemns the influence on a very young girl, who has not been carefully educated and the impatience of parents to ''part from a beloved daughter, reared with fondness at least, if not with wisdom, to a man of whose principles they have any doubt, and of whose mind they have a mean opinion' (p.130). She voices an explanation for this through her protagonist, Mr. Stanley, who states that 'when girls are continually hearing what an advantageous, what a desirable marriage such a young friend has made, with a man so rich, so splendid, so great; though they have been accustomed to hear this very man condemned for his profligacy, perhaps at least they know him to be destitute of piety – when they hear that these things are not considered as any great objection to the union, what opinion must these girls form not only of the maxims by which the world is governed, but of the truth of that religion which these persons profess?' (p.130). This places in a nutshell all that Brontë illustrates through Rosalie Murray and Helen Huntingdon, and tells us a great deal of her struggles to instruct the Robinson girls not to act in such a way. Rosalie, ill-informed and conditioned to accept Sir Thomas Ashby, does not even question the sense of the match. More's Lucilla, however, is well equipped to resist, for she loves reading the Bible, praying regularly to have enough strength to resist sin, and practises self-examination 'to detect every latent evil in her heart' (p.145). She does not attempt to show her cleverness, as does one of More's foils for Lucilla, a wealthy, but over-knowledgeable and hence still unmarried lady of forty-five years of age, Miss Sparkes. Although Miss Sparkes has a considerable fortune, she has remained single because of her forthright use of wit and her being known as 'an Amazon', 'a scholar, and a huntress – a politician and a farmer'. She bears a certain resemblance to Brontë's Matilda Murray in her ability to outride men, consort with grooms and even pick up fearlessly the hind leg of her lame horse. Charles sums up what More thinks is true learning for a lady as being 'a knowledge that is rather detected than displayed, that is felt in its effects on her mind and conversation . . . by the delicacy of her taste, and the correctness of her sentiments' (p.218), certainly not what Miss Sparkes was offering. Brontë evidently does not approve of such a show of cleverness and, following More's lead, advocates virtues such as sincerity and humility depicted in her governess, who attempts to live out such a life-style. As regards what women should learn, Brontë, again like More, even promotes the learning of Latin by girls, a subject she had learned, along with Branwell, from her father, and she takes back to the Robinsons' household, in January 1844, a copy of R. Valpy's *Delectus Sententarium et Historiarum (1842)* in order to teach Edmund Robinson, or more probably the Robinson girls, Latin. More suggests that the reason women are frivolous is because 'the things they are taught are not solid enough to fix the attention, exercise the intellect, and fortify the understanding. They learn little that inures to reasoning or compels to patient meditation' (p.202). This smacks of Wollstonecraft's attitude towards the need for woman to exercise her power to reason, for More, as Wollstonecraft's contemporary, was undoubtedly aware of her ideas.

Charles, after showing great caution and not proceeding too quickly in asking Lucilla to be his wife, in answer to a promise he has made to Mr. Stanley, finally proposes to this lovely, high principled, moral and intellectual young lady, representative of More's ideal woman, well educated but still a modest, domestic being. Mr. Flam describes Lucilla as 'a pattern daughter' who will make 'a pattern wife' (p.246), fulfilling the old proverb that 'Parents are patterns',[46] for she is most certainly a product of her parents. Charles does not rush into asking her to be his wife, which is very like Mr. Weston's approach to Agnes, and he and Lucilla decide to educate their children 'in a conformity of Christian principles' (*Coelebs*, p.224), as do Edward and Agnes Weston. Indeed, Edward Weston, seems to do exactly what More's conduct book suggests and, having fallen in love with a virtuous, upright female, does not propose to her immediately after having found her. Instead, using caution, he awaits the propitious moment, in order to test out whether her principles meet with his strongly Evangelical ones, before committing himself to her. It is an entirely different story in *The Tenant*, where Anne Brontë points out through Helen the folly of allowing one's emotional involvement to control one's decision, and, contrary to all common sense, to rush into marrying someone totally unsuitable from a spiritual point of view. In *Coelebs*, Lucilla is seen to be strong enough to resist the advances of Lord Staunton, a 'rakish' suitor, and to reject him even though he promises to reform if she will become his wife. As a result of being truly devout and well-informed of the problems of male domination and oppression of women in marriages, in which the woman has not made an informed choice, Lucilla proves knowledgeable enough to reply: 'I will never add to the number of those rash women who have risked their eternal happiness on this vain hope'.[47] She refuses her suitor because she listens to her heart and also to the advice of her friend, Mrs. Henrietta Carlton, unlike Helen, who refuses to listen to her aunt's doubts or to those of her friend, Milicent, both of whom strongly advise her against marrying Huntingdon. Henrietta tells Lucilla that Lord Staunton 'had seduced the innocent daughter of one of his tenants, under the most specious pretence of honourable love. This, together with the looseness of his religious principles, leads her to give his lordship a positive refusal' (p.144). Apparently, Lucilla had also refused another man whom she knew she could not love, although he was eminently suitable in other ways. She, desirous of sparing his feelings before he actually offered his hand to her, stops him in advance. Not for her is the vanity of 'seeking to make conquests' (p.144), as we see revealed in the way Rosalie deals with Mr. Hatfield. Lucilla even informs Lord Staunton why she is refusing his hand replying honestly, but courteously, that 'she feared his principles were not those of a man, with whom she could venture to trust her own' (p.156). Interestingly, he responds by telling her that her charming society will reform him and raise his principles and even change his character: just as we see in Brontë's second novel where Helen mistakenly thinks that she too can reform Huntingdon by her principles and society. Helen exhibits no such thorough a knowledge of her age as does Lucilla and is used by Brontë to reveal the great need for the women of her times to be trained to reason and to reflect more deeply on such important matters. Helen typifies the Victorian woman who is convinced of her ability to reform her husband once she is married. Consequently, she incurs the risk of being corrupted by him and thereby losing her eternal happiness, a danger of which Lucilla seems very aware. One of the fallacies of Brontë's day is shown up by her: that women are 'angels in the house',[48] or innocence idealised with the ability to save men by their spiritual qualities, and thereby capable of reforming their husbands. The balance of relationships of that age is challenged by Brontë. The notion that God can civilise through the woman and bring redemption for a worldly husband was indeed a very Victorian faith conviction. In *The Tenant*, Brontë points out the great risk of this unfounded belief, showing through Helen's failure to change her husband that it is God alone who can transform hearts. Brontë's heroine is seen to be unable to escape from her heartless monster of a husband because of the laws of the land, which do not allow wife-instigated divorce or separation except in extreme circumstances of incest or bigamy. Brontë agrees whole-heartedly with More on this question of education and asserts, like her, not, however, from any political viewpoint, that women need to be taught to reason in order to make an informed judgment along Christian lines. In *The Tenant*, Esther Hargrave, educated along these lines by Helen and by Esther's sister, Milicent, finds courage enough to refuse her mother's choice of suitor, because she knows she can never love nor respect him.

More prized a woman's 'heroic fortitude, Christian humility, unshaken trust in God, and submission to his dispensations' as the greatest fruits of such an education,[49] which qualities Brontë used as her ideal in her novels. Indeed, *Coelebs* can be viewed as the embodiment of More's social reaction against late eighteenth-century feminism, which is enshrined by Wollstonecraft's writings, and a major influence upon Brontë's thinking.

Influence of Mary Brunton

Mary Brunton (1778-1818), like Hannah More, was yet another best-selling author of her day who influenced Anne Brontë's writings. According to Jane Austen, Brunton's novel, *Self-Control*, (1810) was 'without anything of nature or probability in it'.[50] Most certainly this is true, not only of *Self-Control*, but also of a later novel she wrote, *Discipline* (1815), where a series of fantastic misadventures stretch one's credulity to the extremes. Whilst Brontë does not share Brunton's propensity for depicting events in such an unreal way in her novels, there remain great similarities, for example, of aim, for More, Brunton and then Brontë all set out in true Evangelical fashion to impart moral guidance to their public in an entertaining manner. In *Self-Control*, Brunton's heroine, Laura, although portrayed as far more beautiful than Agnes Grey, resembles her in her 'unimpeachable manners and morals'. Laura, as do both Agnes and Helen, continually examines her conscience using the Gospel as her reference point, in order to maintain her moral strength, and uphold her Christian behaviour. In addition, one of Brunton's male characters in *Self-Control* bears the same name as Hargrave in *The Tenant,* and also has similar character traits. Brunton's Colonel Hargrave is a victim of his upbringing, being 'the spoiled child of a weak mother (p.185), just as is Walter Hargrave. Indeed, both seem to be graphic examples of how a child ought not to be reared. The ending of *Self-Control* is interesting in that it echoes the sentiment of the ending of *Agnes Grey*, for Laura, happily married at last, is reticent to speak of the domestic joys which she is now experiencing as a result of her 'chastened affection, tempered desires, useful employment and devout meditation,' which 'must be felt – they cannot be described'. This is rather like Agnes's reserved feelings on the subject of her domestic happiness: 'And now I think I have said sufficient' (p.302). Brontë has done her utmost to accomplish her aim, her warnings have been issued and her fictional heroine can now relax in the private world of her domestic bliss.

In Brunton's novel, *Discipline,* with its sequence of events in true Romantic style and love of Edinburgh and the Highlands, we see a serious study of a change gradually being effected in the heroine, Ellen Percy, from the state of her being vain and pretentious to her becoming a devout, reflective, loving and kind wife and mother. This bears resemblance to Brontë's novels in terms of its narrative style, its sentiments on parenting and also in the change in Rosalie, and more particularly in Matilda, brought about by Agnes's educational programme.

Narrated in the first person by Ellen, with some third person narrative interventions in mainly dialogue form, the novel is innovative for its times, as was to be *Agnes Grey,* written nearly forty years later, which is also narrated in the first person by Agnes, with rare authorial interventions. Narrating in the first person allowed Brontë the freedom to personalize her own thoughts, feelings and experiences without stating them to be her own, and allowed her to attribute them to the fictional heroes and heroines of her novels. Consequently, her non-exaggerated descriptions and restrained vocabulary take on a certain reality akin to life, whereas in Mary Brunton's novel, the succession of sensational events lends a certain unreality to her illustrations.

Discipline is similar, to *Agnes Grey* in terms of its intent and character-portrayal. Its very first chapter begins with a quotation from Walter Scott,

'I was wayward, bold, and wild;
A self-willed imp; a grandame's child;
But, half a plague and half a jest,
Was still endured, beloved, carest'

which could easily have been the way in which Anne Brontë could
have described the attitude in childhood of her brother, Branwell, or,
in fictional terms, that of an uncontrollable pupil such as Tom
Bloomfield, whose parents doted nevertheless on his every action, or
how Arthur Huntingdon or any of his merry band of men in *The
Tenant* might well have described their relationship with their
parents when they were children. *Discipline* describes vividly how
Ellen Percy is brought up by indulgent parents who allow her an over-
abundance of liberties, and never prevent her from getting her own
way. Consequently, Ellen is unable to cope with the world, having to
learn, instead, through the tragic events which befall her, how to
become a woman of integrity. Brunton's method of teaching by giving
the reader all the entertainment and adventure needed as a ploy to
continue to read the book bears close resemblance with Anne Brontë's
method of subject presentation, although Brunton's adventures,
which are incredibly wild and sensational, depart almost entirely
from the reality of Brontë's portrayal, in *Agnes Grey,* of ordinary day-
to-day events in which her naughty charges get involved. Brunton, far
more didactic, speaks frequently through her use of third person
interventions to tell her readers how such bad behaviour can lead to
sin. Ellen is brought up by doting, wealthy parents on whom the
mother 'exercised a control too gentle over a spirit which needed to be
reined by a firmer hand than hers'. This led to Ellen becoming 'proud,
petulant, and rebellious', faults which could be traced to her never
having been called on to 'pay the natural penalties of impatience or
self-indulgence'.[51] Because she was 'but a child' (p.5) all was allowed.
As a consequence, Ellen becomes arrogant, self-willed, impatient of
reproof, loving of flattery and sway and, what is more, one of the most
unhappy of beings. Brontë seems to have imitated this way of
portraying effects, which can be seen through her serious but also
amusing illustrations of indiscipline. Yet, rather than spell out
everything in detail as does Brunton, she allows the consequences of
such actions on the lives of the pupil, governess and parents simply to
emerge. Examples of this occur when Agnes is confronted by the
undisciplined Tom Bloomfield, and also when she is tricked and
deceived by Rosalie and Matilda Murray, for, in both cases, Brontë
reveals the two sides of the events to ensure that the reader, through
his intelligent comprehension, is aware of the truth of the situation
without her having to intervene directly in the novel.

Brontë's Rosalie Murray, educated only enough to present herself well and attract a rich husband, greatly resembles Brunton's example of Miss Juliet Arnold, a girl 'educated to be married' (p.16), and a product of the 'Mahometan Education' mentioned by More, and therefore taught only those accomplishments which are felt necessary to attract the notice and admiration of men. Rosalie's marriage turns out as badly as does Juliet's tragic elopement with Lord Glendower, although eventually Juliet's son is accepted as the rightful heir. The character of Mrs. Percy's friend, Miss Mortimer, who cares for Ellen after her mother dies, resembles both Brontë's own Aunt Branwell and Helen Graham/Huntingdon's Aunt Maxwell, upright and high principled as both of them are portrayed. She also bears similarity to Agnes Grey herself. Ellen's description of Miss Mortimer's method of dealing with her own and Juliet's occasionally malicious practical jokes could well be a description of Agnes's way of dealing with her naughty pupils, firmly sticking to her course of action whatever the pressure upon her and only offering advice by example. Ellen says: 'she was never officious, and was even so sparing of direct advice, that, had she not been the most humble of human beings, I should have said that she trusted to the dignity and grace of her general sentiments, and the beautiful consistency of her example, for effecting the enormous transition from what I was to what I ought to be.' (pp.20/21)

Another example of Brunton's influence on Brontë can be seen in her choice of heroes, such as the man Ellen eventually marries, Maitland/Henry Graham, who is undoubtedly a solid, dependable man of sense and integrity. Indeed, he is very like Mr. Weston or even Gilbert Markham, although he is depicted as much more sensational and larger than life than Brontë's more down-to-earth heroes. Ellen's first attempt at working as a governess is with a Mrs. Murray, a name also used by Anne Brontë for Agnes's second post. Brunton, in describing what governesses do, expresses similar sentiments to those of all the Brontë sisters on this condition of a governess, labelling it as being 'little removed from servitude' (p.211). There are many other similarities, apart from that of using the same surnames, Graham and Murray, for example. Ellen, who becomes greatly impoverished by losing all her fortune when her father commits suicide, is compelled to utilise her skills to sell 'the little ingenious works' which she has learned to make at her fashionable boarding school. To help her earn enough money to live she is reduced to selling these self-made objects, just as Helen Huntingdon, once she has left the financial security of her married home, has to sell her own paintings to pay the bills. Another likeness worthy of note is that Brunton's definition of education, 'learning what is afterwards to be useful' (p.190), is exactly along the same lines as regards tone and sentiment as is Brontë's.

Influence of Mary Wollstonecraft

Whether Anne Brontë, Mary Brunton or Hannah More actually read Wollstonecraft's works remains somewhat unclear. However, Wollstonecraft was certainly so well known to her contemporaries that everyone might well have read her in secret, but no-one would have wanted to admit to the fact. Her unsavoury life-style and chequered existence with various lovers meant that her works, although recognised as brilliant, would not readily have been found in the sort of libraries frequented by Anne Brontë. Wollstonecraft was even called 'a hyena in petticoats' by Horace Walpole.[52] In any case, it would not have been politic to confess a knowledge of her works, which were considered as lacking in respectability right up to the late nineteenth century. Yet, for all this, one cannot deny that there are distinct echoes from Wollstonecraft's writings to be found in Brontë's novels, although neither Brontë, More nor Brunton would have wished to be associated with her radically political and subversive feminist intention.[53]

In Wollstonecraft's earlier writings, such as *Mary, A Fiction (1788)*, her mocking style of saying one thing, whilst meaning another, reminds us of Brontë's wry humour. From the very first chapter, where we meet Eliza, Mary's mother, and are told that she has 'a kind of indolence in her temper, which might be termed negative good-nature: her virtues, indeed, were all of that stamp. She carefully attended to the *shews* of things, and her opinions, I should have said prejudices, were such as the generality approved of',[54] we can see a resemblance between her style and Brontë's. All is recounted by Wollstonecraft in a 'tongue in cheek' manner, and imitated by Brontë in *Agnes Grey*, especially in her account of Uncle Robson, Mrs. Bloomfield's brother, where her true meaning can be understood from her dryly humorous statements, showing her preference for the use of understatement to allow her convictions to emerge: 'He was a thick-set, strongly-built man, but he had found some means of compressing his waist into a remarkably small compass, and that, together with the unnatural stiffness of his form, showed that the lofty-minded, manly Mr. Robson, the scorner of the female sex, was not above the foppery of stays' (AG, p.75). Wollstonecraft points out the dangerous effects of Eliza's reading novels, revealing, in her ironic tone, her dislike of young women spending time on such activities as 'sentimental novels' which 'dwelt on the love-scenes which encouraged her sweet tears of sensibility' She goes on to mock novel-reading rather prettily saying of Eliza 'had she thought while she read, her mind would have been contaminated' (p.3, *Mary*). Such an attitude of mind evidently influenced Brontë's portrayal of Rosalie Murray, who is also seen to spend an inordinate amount of time on novel-reading, which undoubtedly influenced her selfish attitude towards men and her conviction that it was through her personal attractions, rather than by her inner qualities that she would achieve many conquests. In both cases, Eliza's and Rosalie's education was based on 'superficial accomplishments' and lack of solid 'duties for her to fulfil' (p.2, *Mary*). In Eliza's case, this meant that she never thought for herself and therefore readily submitted to marrying 'a vicious fool', as in duty bound. Again just the same attitude of mind as Rosalie's, when she agrees to marry an equally 'vicious fool', without giving too much thought to the 'transaction', other than to assure herself that Sir Thomas Ashby would offer her in return wealth and an estate. As Eliza grew up, Wollstonecraft reveals the bad effects upon her of a lack of maternal tenderness. This idea is used by Brontë in many of her examples and is especially true of Mrs. Murray's attitude to her daughters, for her only interest in them is to marry them off well. Rosalie Murray, once married and mother of a baby girl, for whom she feels nothing, (just like Wollstonecraft's Eliza, who has no real affection for her daughter, Mary), typifies the ill-informed, upper-class woman described by both Wollstonecraft and Brontë, who, never having been taught to work at any relationship as she grows up, and having been inveigled into an unhappy arranged marriage to satisfy her parents' greed, is intent only on self-pleasure. Having received no affection, she can feel none for mankind, and can therefore give none to her offspring, unlike Wollstonecraft who, even when travelling to Scandinavia chose to be accompanied by Fanny, her daughter by Gilbert Imlay.

Wollstonecraft mocks the way in which girls are brought up, suggesting that Mary, the daughter of Eliza, is better off in having had her education neglected by her mother, whose lack of interest in her has caused her to have to reason for herself and thereby to find a faith in God: 'Neglected in every respect, and left to the operations of her own mind, she considered every thing that came under her inspection, and learned to think and also to believe in angels and heaven' (p.4, *Mary*). Left to her own devices, Mary has learned self-control, even how to curb her anger and impatience to save herself from 'cruel remorse' (p.5, *Mary*). This can also be seen in *Agnes Grey*, where Rosalie and Matilda, who, conditioned by their mother to accept certain outcomes as their duty and their destiny, are subjected by her to the wrong sort of education, (prior to Agnes's input), as was Mary's mother, Eliza, and cannot therefore avoid the disastrous consequences brought about by their inability to think or reason for themselves. Mary has learned household management from witnessing her mother's faults and inattention to both herself and to her servants, which inspires some of Brontë's examples. One illustration she gives shows how Mrs. Bloomfield, who treats her governess much worse than Agnes's mother treats her kitchen maid, has very poor skills in that direction and does not watch over her staff or successfully choose meals which please her husband. Mr. Bloomfield reacts badly to what he deems her lack of management and goes round swearing at all his employees and treating his wife very badly, even in front of Agnes, their newly arrived governess.

Another similarity exists between both authors in their concern with arranged marriages. This can be seen in Wollstonecraft's Mary, who, although she has managed to acquire many qualities of mind in her neglected upbringing, still gives in to her father's desire to marry her off to Charles, in order to pacify his worries over the disputes of their two estates. Rosalie, not as well-informed as Mary, also agrees to marry a man she does not love, for material reasons. Mary acquiesces to her father's request, not for material gain, but rather because she is pressurized by him to marry that very day for fear that her extremely ill mother should die before the wedding. The same night as Mary pronounces 'the awful vow without thinking of it' (p.13, *Mary*) to marry a man she does not know or love, her mother does indeed die. Once married, Mary travels with her friend, Anne, to Portugal, where she meets with two gentlemen and three fashion-conscious young ladies. Wollstonecraft reveals her contempt for the way in which the fashion of the day was to teach modern languages merely for showy reasons, saying that all that was absorbed from such reading was 'Hamlet will tell you – words – words' (p.24, *Mary*). Wollstonecraft states that the qualities needed by a young woman are more a good appearance 'and above all, her genius, and cultivation of mind.' Written in the third person narrative, this early work of fiction shows Wollstonecraft's great interest in sensibility à la Rousseau, confronting problems in fiction and in life, which had been absorbed by Wollstonecraft's imagination. Her disappointment at the outcome of the French Revolution causes a change of heart on her part towards Rousseau. Claire Tomalin points out how much Wollstonecraft abhorred his suggestion that educated women would lose their power over men, for her desire was not for them 'to have power over men, but over themselves.' (*Life and Death of Mary Wollstonecraft*. p.108).

Brontë is even more influenced by Wollstonecraft's *The Wrongs of Woman: or Maria A Fragment,* her second work of fiction, which she began in 1796, and which was not published until 1798, the year after she died. In this novel, Wollstonecraft shows her concern to exhibit 'the misery and oppression, peculiar to women, that arise out of the partial laws and customs of society' *(Preface).* This can be seen in her portrayal of Jemima, the wardress of the mental asylum, in which Maria is imprisoned. Jemima has been totally oppressed by society through the misfortune of her birth and upbringing 'and loved not her fellow-creatures, because she had never been beloved' (*The Wrongs of Woman*, p.82).

Wollstonecraft was especially conscious of 'matrimonial despotism of heart and conduct' and the oppression of all classes of women, which she blamed on their lack of information: 'the wrongs of different classes of women, equally oppressive, though, from the difference of education, necessarily various' (p.74). Brontë is certainly inspired by this theme of matrimonial oppression and lack of good education, which she traces in her second novel, where Helen faces great unhappiness and suffers at the hands of her husband, after making an ill-informed choice of marriage partner. Wollstonecraft's narrative recounts how her fictional heroine, Maria, whom we meet from the onset, confined to a cell, deprived of her relatively new-born baby, has been placed there by her husband in an attempt, on his part, to get possession of her estate. He has also been responsible for wresting their baby daughter from her 'who had been entrapped, kidnapped, in the most fraudulent manner' (p.83, *The Wrongs of Woman*). More influence of Rousseau is evident here as Wollstonecraft reveals that Maria is breast-feeding her baby, much advocated in his *Emile*. Suckling was, apparently, the fashion amongst radicals and, according to Claire Tomalin, Wollstonecraft's friend, Roscoe, had enormous success with his translation of *The Nurse*, a long Italian poem, which praised it greatly. As the tale emerges, Maria meets up with a fellow inmate of the lunatic asylum called Henry Darnford, whom she feels she has met previously. Apparently, Maria, who had been married for her money, having spent five years paying off her husband's debts and seeing him ruin his health and appearance through drink and womenizing, eventually attempted to flee to France with her baby daughter. This is not unlike what happens to Helen as regards the husband and the flight, although it remains puzzling why Huntingdon married Helen instead of Annabella Wilmot, a vastly wealthier heiress, unless, of course, Brontë wants us to suppose that Annabella refused him, preferring the title of Lady Lowborough and realizing that a future dalliance with Huntingdon would not be impossible. Here the resemblance between Brontë's and Wollstonecraft's themes ends, for Maria, drugged by her French maid, awakens, as mentioned, to find herself in an even more nightmarish situation, imprisoned in an asylum, evocatively called 'a Mansion of despair' (p.45), minus her daughter. This episode is more like Mary Brunton's *Discipline*, published later in 1815, where the sick Ellen Percy, also having been drugged, wakes up to find herself in a mental asylum. Wollstonecraft depicts Maria as a rational being with certain rights of her own, able to leave her husband, take on a new lover and even to claim divorce. This is far more forceful a representation than Brontë's portrayal of Helen, who leaves Arthur, not because she feels she has the right to do so, but because she cannot, as a loving parent, stand by and continue to watch the corruption of her child's soul.

However, the greatest similarity between the two authors is one of narrative style. Wollstonecraft's *Wrongs of Woman* begins with an account of Maria's imprisonment and we, the readers, meet her for the first time at a point in her life when many events (unknown to us at this stage) have already taken place, leading to her imprisonment. As Volume 2 of the novel begins, we are presented with Maria's memoirs, which have been written as a first person account, embedded in the novel, and incorporated there to allow Maria's background and sufferings to be known by Henry Darnford and by Jemima. Maria's intent in writing them is to 'instruct her daughter, and shield her from the misery, the tyranny, her mother knew not how to avoid' (p.82, *The Wrongs of Woman*), and to leave her guide-lines to help her avoid her mother's fate. Her anxiety over her little girl and the fact that her husband is not the sort of father in whose hands she feels content to leave her child 'if she thought of her daughter, it was to wish that she had a father whom her mother could respect and love' (p.90, *The Wrongs of Woman)* is reflected in Brontë's portrayal of Helen's feelings about little Arthur's father, and how she wished he were different for the sake of her child. Wollstonecraft insists, in this work, on emphasising the ills of being born a girl in her generation, as is evident from Maria's request to Jemima to help her retrieve her baby daughter so that she may 'give her an education' and 'prepare her body and mind to encounter the ills which await her sex' (p.121, *The Wrongs of Woman).* She even says, 'Why was I not born a man, or why was I born at all?' (p.139, End of Volume 1, *The Wrongs of Woman*). After falling in love with Darnford and, through Jemima's help, discovering that her child is dead, Maria determines to allow Darnford to learn of her background through reading her memoirs, in order to inform him of all the past events leading to her marriage and to her entry into the asylum. The memoirs end with crossed-out references to Darnford (and to Jemima), which are intended by Maria to prevent their knowing her thoughts on them. This is so like *The Tenant,* where we are introduced to Helen at a point in her life when what has befallen her is unknown to Gilbert Markham and also to us, the readers. Then comes the embedded journal, which is also written in the first person and gives an account of Helen's upbringing and background. The diary ends with torn-out pages to prevent Gilbert from knowing what she thought of him. The novel then resumes with the letter of Gilbert. Unfortunately, Wollstonecraft died before *The Wrongs of Woman* was completely finished and it is therefore difficult to conclude on what would have been the final arrangement of the novel. However, the striking coincidence of both authors using a starting point where the heroine's past is entirely unknown, followed by an embedded account, in which the 'hero' learns of the tragic events affecting the heroine and comes to a complete understanding of her great sufferings, is worthy of note. Through the use of this same narrative technique, the first person account in diary or memoirs form is handed to the 'lover' in question.

One difference of approach between Brontë and Wollstonecraft is that the latter discredits the idea of the sanctity of marriage, which she feels interferes with woman's independence. In *The Wrongs of Woman,* she states: 'The marriage state is certainly that in which women, generally speaking, can be most useful; but I am far from thinking that a woman, once married, ought to consider the engagement as indissoluble (especially if there be no children to reward her for sacrificing her feelings) in case her husband merits neither her love, nor esteem.' She continues by saying that no woman should have to stay with a man 'for whom she can cherish neither affection nor esteem, or even be of any use to him' for such 'is an abjectness of condition, the enduring of which no concurrence of circumstances can ever make a duty in the sight of God or just men' (p.157, *The Wrongs of Woman*). In *The Tenant,* we see Helen ceasing to love or esteem her husband or even to be useful to him and eventually resolving to leave him. However, unlike Wollstonecraft's philosophy on marriage, which can be seen portrayed in Maria's encouragement of Darnford's attentions whilst her husband is still alive, Brontë's is such that Helen, in heart and mind, is still wedded before God to Arthur Huntingdon, and, as such, cannot entertain Gilbert Markham as her lover, until such time as her husband dies. Once Arthur becomes ill, Helen fulfills her duty as wife and returns to Grassdale to nurse him, placing her marriage vows and her vocation to help him to repent and attain eternal life well above her selfish aims for earthly happiness. To Wollstonecraft, independence for women is the essence of her feminism, and, although she did agree to marry William Godwin clandestinely, she still viewed marriage as simply a property transaction where the woman renounced all rights to her assets. This was decidedly true for her day and Brontë shares her views to some extent in *The Tenant,* where Helen's money is seen to be entirely at Huntingdon's disposal. Yet, in *The Tenant,* Brontë was certainly not putting forward Wollstonecraft's political point of view in favour of equal rights before the law for women, for she was far more concerned with the reality of the situation and how such problems could be resolved by a more personal intervention. She felt that the solution lay in the fact that a woman needed a good education to help her be able to reflect on all the options available to her and, if asked for in marriage, to make a wise and sensible choice of husband. To Brontë, marriage is celebrated by two individuals before God, and is a holy institution. Although she felt certain reservations about marriages where the law inhibited wronged women like Helen Huntingdon from acting independently, forcing them to be treated as chattels and incapable of any independent action, Brontë shows, even in such situations as these, how enterprising are her ideas. She comes up with the idea of 'necessity being the mother of invention', and describes how Helen manages to get Arthur to sign a legally witnessed paper which allows her to be in sole charge of her child.

Brontë suggests that when a marriage is founded on truth and goodness it can succeed and illustrates this in *The Tenant* by juxtaposing the good and sensible marriage of Gilbert and Helen against Helen's earlier failed union with Arthur where, along with the debauchery of the husband, the constant lack of truthful communication between them has broken down the marital relationship. Losing one's property in marriage seems not as important an issue to her as to Wollstonecraft. Helen is seen to lose all her assets, but Brontë appears to suggest that, as long as a marriage is founded on love and mutual respect before God, it is natural that a woman should hand over her belongings to her partner for their walk ahead.

However, Brontë does agree with Wollstonecraft that marriage is not the only way in which a woman can be fulfilled. She shows this both in her own life and also in *Agnes Grey*, where her heroine, Agnes, manages to achieve relative happiness by hard work in her mother's school. It is only after doing her duty that Brontë allows Agnes to find that inner contentment of a love marriage with Mr. Weston. Wollstonecraft reacts far more than does Brontë against the idea of the times that a girl with an intellectual education would find it extremely hard to get a husband. On talking of girls' education, Wollstonecraft states 'Reading, writing and arithmetic and French, painting, watercolours or music', but certainly not 'good sense' are the subjects needed for the marriage market, where 'any sign of an independent intellect . . . could prove a positive hindrance'.[55] Some blame for this attitude, prevalent in the eighteenth and early nineteenth centuries, can be attributed to Dr. Gregory's conduct book, *A Father's Legacy to his daughters'* (1774), which was treated by Wollstonecraft with some severity in her *Vindication of the Rights of Woman, (Chapt.v, Section iii)*. Dr. Gregory advised women to keep their learning 'a profound secret' otherwise it could severely hamper their chances of finding a husband. Although Brontë shared Wollstonecrafts's desire for women to develop their capacities for reasoning, she saw no necessity for girls to broadcast their learning, agreeing rather with Hannah More that they should learn useful subjects, including domestic management, but keep silent whenever necessary and never thrust their views on men. Wollstonecraft states that girls were expected to 'have been well, or at least fashionably educated' for if they were left without a fortune, they 'must frequently remain single'.[56]

Brontë also reacts against the materialistic attitude of marrying for money and position in her novels, and gives a picture of a society bent on fashion and appearances, where parents are more concerned with what others think about their children than what their children are really like or what they are taught. Her example of Mr. Bloomfield's constantly telling Agnes to see that his children are made 'decent' and caring little for their or Agnes's feelings, is a particularly vivid one. Brontë follows Wollstonecrafts's lead here, sharing her view that women, who are often badly educated from childhood and have never been taught to work at relationships as they grow up, lean rather too heavily on the idea that only beauty and marriage matter in life, rather than instruction as to how to become rational, independent and useful, qualities which both writers maintain are the essence of future woman. This viewpoint is inspired by Wollstonecraft's certitude that women need useful occupations as much as men do, to keep them from acting irrationally out of boredom. She comments: 'how difficult it was for women to avoid growing romantic, who have no active duties or pursuits' (p.87, *The Wrongs of Woman*), a theme on which she had elaborated in her *Vindication of the Rights of Woman* (Chapt xiii, Section 2).

Contrary to the literary norm of her age, Brontë depicts in her first novel a hard-working, conscientious, ordinary, and somewhat plain, well-educated girl, who marries for love, without possessing a dowry, and who is accepted as the equal of her husband, both in intellectual ability and in integrity. Brontë reveals briefly to her readers Agnes and Edward Weston settling down together after having given much cautious thought to the subject, producing children and leading a happy life, based entirely on Christian principles. Yet Brontë goes even further, for she encourages her readers to think that the children of such a union, parented in this positive way, would, in their turn, grow up as independent, Christian-thinking adults able to adopt a rational approach to life, like Agnes herself, and be equipped to pass on such knowledge to their children.

Although Brontë's examples of successful marriages come mostly from middle-class families (like that of her fictional Agnes and Edward), and her failures from the aristocracy and landed gentry (like Lord and Lady Lowborough's, Mr. and Mrs. Bloomfield's, and Arthur and Helen Huntingdon's), she is not just echoing

Wollstonecraft's opinion of upper-class decadence and double standards, gained whilst a governess to Lady Kingsborough's children and also shown fictionally in *The Wrongs of Woman* by Jemima's attitude to a man whom she had met in the household of the person whose mistress she was. Apparently, often in her master's society, this man had 'descanted on the evils which arise in society from the despotism of rank and riches' (p.114, *The Wrongs of Woman*), but as soon as Jemima was forced to beg him for help after her master's death, he had refused and replied to her request with the rather trite phrase: 'every person willing to work may find employment'. Brontë shares Wollstonecraft's antipathy to such double standards and points out the necessity for *all* families – middle-class or aristocratic – to carefully instil social responsibilities and a solid Christian code of morals into their children, so that they may pass on such skills in due course. Granted, there does exist a bias on Brontë's part towards examples like Agnes's own parents, or Mrs. Markham, wife of a gentleman farmer, whose occupations are seen to have kept them from a life of idleness, which she personifies in Arthur Huntingdon's and Walter Hargrave's way of living. Brontë more than hints that marriages between people of the middle-classes are based more on common sense and solid values than on the desire for fashion, money and social position. Consequently, better relationships between parents and offspring exist there than is usual in aristocratic circles. This does not differ greatly from Wollstonecraft's attitude as expressed in her *Original Stories from Real Life: with Conversations Calculated to Regulate the Affections and Form the Mind to Truth and Goodness (1788),* where Mrs. Mason is responsible for educating two wealthy orphans, Mary (14 years) and Caroline (12 years), whose selfishness and desire to gratify instantly their every desire, without ever thinking of the consequences, is viewed by Wollstonecraft as part of *'an aristocratic culture'.*[57] This attitude, Wollstonecraft had seen in Lady Kingsborough and can be seen reflected in Brontë's Huntingdon and even, to some extent, in Brontë's brother, Branwell. Such selfishness and bad behaviour are also reflected in *Agnes Grey,* in Brontë's depiction of the young Bloomfields and the antics of Agnes's two pupils, Rosalie and Matilda Murray. In the preface of *Original Stories from Real Life,* Wollstonecraft notes how one cannot expect children to behave morally when their parents lack the education necessary to guide them: 'to wish that parents would, themselves, mould the ductile passions, is a chimerical wish, for the present generation have their own passions to combat with, and fastidious pleasures to pursue, neglecting those pointed out by nature: we must therefore pour premature knowledge into the succeeding one; and, teaching virtue, explain the nature of vice. Cruel necessity'.

Anne Brontë says much the same thing in *Agnes Grey*.

Wollstonecraft also uses a female narrator in the first person, her protagonist, Mrs. Mason, for her *Original Stories (1788)* and, as already stated, for her fiction *The Wrongs of Woman (1798)*. This technique was extremely innovative especially for 1788 and was tried by Wollstonecraft even earlier than Mary Brunton's attempt at first-person female narration in her novels. Brontë follows this in *Agnes Grey*, which in many ways is also a conduct book in disguise. The way in which Mrs. Mason manages to effect some changes in her charges' behaviour and attitude to the poor is also imitated in the techniques adopted by Agnes, for example her visits to the cottagers with the two girls to help them to realise how fortunate they are. However Mrs. Mason seems to achieve far more of a reduction in her charges' selfishness as a consequence of her visits than does Agnes.

As already stated the episode where Mrs. Mason crushes the head of a lark with her foot rather than see it suffer greatly resembles Agnes's killing the birds given to Tom Bloomfield, rather than her letting him torture them for both books use as their protagonists women who apply discipline and reason to their daily lives.

In *A Vindication of the Rights of Woman (1792)*, 'a conduct – book model of rational, domestic and 'chaste motherhood', Wollstonecraft emphasises the need for men and women to be considered as equals, not just in intellectual matters but also in the political and financial fields. She does not want women to be viewed as 'ornamental dolls: fragile, flirtatious and helpless',[58] who must have a dowry to seal any marriage deal. Female independence is the essence of her feminism. By the nineteenth century the emphasis on woman's place had shifted away from this merely decorative role to woman being viewed as an ideal, possessed of redemptive qualities and at the moral centre of the family – some sort of domestic goddess – but still not capable of, nor trained to have, any independence of thought. Brontë supports strongly the idea that women should aim to be more independent, and certainly does not view them as domestic angels, as is evident from her illustration of Helen's failure to reform Arthur Huntingdon. Her position on women's moral nature and education resembles to a certain degree that of Wollstonecraft's: Women need to be educated 'in the proper and rational exercise of virtue'[59] in order to improve socially through education the minds of children and parents. Wollstonecraft aims at teaching her pupils humanitarian values, whereas Brontë's intent is to instruct them in a Christian code of ethics. In addition, Brontë's naturally restrained manner of writing differs widely from Wollstonecraft's exaggerated frankness of style. To conclude, although Brontë is inspired by Wollstonecraft, it is evident that the *raison d'être* of these two writers remains poles apart.

Influence of Jane Austen

One of the eighteenth-century writers, many of them women, whose balance of reason and passion seemed to influence Brontë was Jane Austen. Although it is difficult to prove that Anne ever read Austen, it seems more than likely that she would have secretly rejected her eldest sister's dislike of the author and would have wanted to ascertain for herself the quality of such a well-known writer's works. Penny Gay asserts that Anne Brontë may well have been *'a closet Jane Austen reader',*[60] citing a similarity of tone, for example between Mr. Boarham's proposal to young Helen Graham and that of Mr. Collins's proposal to Elizabeth Bennet in *Pride and Prejudice.* Given time, George Moore also felt that Anne could well have attained the same, if not even greater, heights than the better-known Jane Austen.

Both authors tend to juxtapose opposites in their novels in order to throw emphasis on the truth of the situation. In *Sense and Sensibility*, Elinor Dashwood and Edward Ferrars represent good sense with Marianne Dashwood and Willoughby representing wild Romantic emotionalism In both Brontë's novels, the same sort of juxtapositioning occurs. In *Agnes Grey*, Agnes, Agnes's mother and Mr. Weston represent loyalty and high principles whereas Rosalie Murray, Sir Thomas Ashby and the Rector, Mr. Hatfield, are on the side of unprincipled self-indulgence. In *The Tenant*, Helen Graham/ Huntingdon and Gilbert Markham are pitted against Annabella Wilmot and Arthur Huntingdon. Another parallel exists between the two authors in Rosalie Murray's acceptance of marriage with Sir Thomas Ashby just for his money and his estate and, in *Mansfield Park*, Maria Bertram's acceptance of Mr. Rushworth for similar reasons. Maria's marriage, is arranged by her interfering Aunt Norris rather than by her mother, the rather indolent, self-interested Lady Bertram, who, without the influence of her husband, away in the West Indies, can only rely on her stronger sister's opinions. Conditioned from childhood, like most young ladies of her age, to accept that it is a girl's duty to marry well, Lady Bertram cannot see any problem to Maria's accepting such a proposal. Maria herself acquiesces without reflection, in contrast with Fanny Price, whose more rational approach and high principles will not allow her to accept the proposal of Henry Crawford, a man she cannot respect, even when her uncle tries his hardest to make her change her mind. Let us hope that Jane Austen, who was unmarried and whose sole contact with children was in the capacity of aunt to her nephews and nieces did not see herself, with her ironic sense of humour, as an Aunt Norris. In *The Tenant,* we also see an aunt with a young niece to marry off. However, this aunt does her best, but in vain, to educate her niece to be able to resist any marriage proposals which come from unprincipled men. Similarly, in

Sense and Sensibility, Marianne Dashwood, allowing her emotions the upper hand, opts for Mr. Willoughby as her suitor. This shows the same lack of reflective thought as that of Helen Graham, whose choice of Arthur Huntingdon also ends in tragedy. Elinor Dashwood, Marianne's sister, manages to control her emotions even when Lucy Steele tells her that she, Lucy, is engaged to Edward Ferrars, the man whom Elinor greatly esteems and believes admires her. Later, when Edward is freed from his commitment by Lucy's deserting him to marry his brother (who has inherited all Edward's former money), Edward proposes to Elinor, and at this point she commits herself whole-heartedly to him, knowing him to be a good man and capable of great loyalty. As a character, Edward Ferrars bears a strong resemblance to Brontë's Edward Weston and even to Gilbert Markham, whose awkwardness is finally overcome by Helen's great love for him, as is that of Edward Ferrars by Elinor's. In *Agnes Grey* we see Agnes saying goodbye to the old house, the well-known garden the little village church which also reflects the tone of Austen's somewhat ironic portrayal of Marianne's farewell to her old home with all its Romantic emotionalism.

Indeed, there are also similarities in Austen's and Brontë's approach to women's education. Both see the need for women to be educated in order to be able to reflect and reason. This is an argument Brontë promotes through Agnes, which can be compared with Jane Austen's portrayal in *Persuasion,* of the voice of reason in the character of Anne Elliot, who draws up a workable plan to help her father, Sir Walter Elliot, to 'retrench' before his financial position at Kellynch Hall gets even worse. Austen's heroine is portrayed as a woman who is no longer an outstanding beauty (yet we must not forget that she caught the attention of her cousin, Mr. Elliot, at Lyme Regis), and is different from the description of slightly more ordinariness which fits Agnes Grey, who, like Anne Elliot, is educated sufficiently to be able to make an independent choice. Even though vastly attracted to her suitor, Captain Wentworth, Anne Elliot accepts reluctantly the advice of Lady Russell, her late mother's friend, and refuses him. She also refuses two more suitors because she does not love them. In the latter case, even though by marrying Mr. Elliot she would have gained her own mother's title of Lady Elliot after her father's death, she would not consent to marry him, for she cannot respect his person. Yet after all, there is a Romantic ending to *Persuasion* (just as there is to *Agnes Grey* and to *The Tenant of Wildfell Hall*), where Anne Elliot takes the second chance she is offered to marry Captain Wentworth, 'a man of sense',[61] in the same way as Helen does when she accepts Gilbert as her second husband. Agnes Grey, who will only consent to marry someone she loves and to whom adherence to Godly principles is of paramount importance, resembles both Anne Elliot, as regards her strength of character, and also Fanny Price in *Mansfield Park*. This is in complete contrast to Fanny's cousin, Maria Bertram, whose marriage, for all the wrong reasons, leads to the utmost misery, as does the union in *Agnes Grey* between Rosalie Murray and Sir Thomas Ashby. Indeed, one has only to look at Brontë's fictional heroines, Agnes and Helen, to recall those of Jane Austen, the principled, devout Fanny Price, the self-controlled Elinor Dashwood or the practical, reflective Anne Elliot.

Jane Austen, although unmarried and childless like Anne Brontë, shows herself to be amazingly understanding of children, possibly because of her involvement with the upbringing of her brother's little daughter, Anna. Indeed, children figure in all six of her completed novels in some capacity or other;[62] yet it is evident that they hold a more symbolic than dramatic role, for the young children in Austen rarely speak, with the exception of ten-year-old Fanny Price who is induced by her cousin Edmund to reply to his kindly questions, and Margaret Dashwood. Margaret endears herself to the readers by her revelatory remarks spoken usually at the wrong moment, as when she informs us that the name of Elinor's beau begins with the letter F and also when she makes the assumption that, because Willoughby has cut a lock of Marianne's hair, they must be engaged. No such charming children exist in Anne's work although Anne valiantly tries to stick up for Rosalie and attributes to her a good disposition but a bad education. However, it is not only Anne Brontë who depicts younger children as seriously undisciplined, for Austen, too, by resorting to irony, gives us many examples of over-indulgent parents allowing their children to commit excruciatingly bad behaviour. This is particularly evident in the scene where Lady Middleton and her children are entertaining not only the Dashwoods but also the Miss Steeles. Lady Middleton seems to be incapable of reprimanding her children and permits them to behave atrociously without scolding them, even praising them instead. Her 'four noisy children' enter the room after dinner 'and pulled her about, tore her clothes, and put an end to every kind of discourse except what related to themselves'.[63] This is very like Brontë's illustration of Mrs. Bloomfield who, when in the act of praising her son, seems oblivious of the fact that, at the same time, he is wiping his dirty hands on her dress in joyful glee. When Lady Middleton's son, John, throws Miss Steele's pocket handkerchief out of the window, we are reminded of the scene in *Agnes Grey* where the marauding Tom and the other Bloomfield children try to throw Agnes's work-box out of the window. Austen's irony knows no bound as we, the readers, witness the goings-on and watch the Miss Steeles submit so readily to this dreadful behaviour in order to ingratiate themselves with their hostess. Even when Lady Middleton is forced to take a screaming child out of the room, Lucy Steele, much to our amusement, carries on this charade with Elinor, declaring the children to be 'a charming little family' on whom she quite dotes already. Elinor's composure in replying with a smile, 'I should guess so from what I have witnessed this morning' (p.58). allows the reader to smile with Elinor in secret complicity. Lucy realises Elinor is too much for her but continues all the same trying desperately to get Elinor to incriminate herself in some rash statement of disapproval. To Lucy's suggestion that Elinor thinks 'the little Middletons rather too much indulged' which she, Lucy, feels is only high spirits for she cannot bear children to be 'tame and quiet', Elinor replies masterfully that, while at Barton Park, she never thinks of 'tame and quiet children with any abhorrence' (p.58). This witty response bears a great resemblance in content to Hannah More's more serious reproach to parents who allow their children to tyrannize the household and monopolize all situations, which reduces the parents to being mere slaves of their offspring. Brontë gives us a similar, lively scene in *Agnes Grey* where this domination of parents by children takes place. On arrival at the Bloomfield's home, Agnes is struck by the imperious nature of the commands of the children to her as the governess and notices how they refuse to obey their elders. She also raises the point that some of the male members of the family, like Uncle Robson, encourage their bad behaviour and exalt in the fact that they are already beyond 'petticoat government'. Brontë is evidently inspired by both Austen and More here but, in such humorous examples, her dry wit more resembles that of Jane Austen's. Another example of how children turn out when subjected to such indulgent treatment can be seen in *Persuasion,* where, at a scene at a children's party at Uppercross, we see the 'riotous boys' and 'chattering girls' who prevent Mr. Musgrove from being heard, even when he speaks 'with a very raised voice' to Lady Russell. The 'clamour of the children on his knees' totally spoils their conversation and once again we see the children monopolize the family. Austen ends this scene with the ironic statement, 'It was a fine family-piece' (p.991), which both amuses her readers and also instructs them as to the truth – exactly as Anne Brontë aimed to do in both her novels. Yet another example of this over-indulgence by parents to their children can be seen in *Pride and Prejudice* where we meet the rather silly, vain mother of the Bennet girls who panders to their appearance but never to their minds, whilst her husband abdicates all responsibility for them, washing his hands of what happens in his selfish pursuit of peace. This almost brings down the family and nearly incurs its dishonour through the Lydia/Wickham episode. Again in *Mansfield*

Park, we see the selfishness and weakness of Lady Maria Bertram and the over-occupation of her husband, Sir Thomas Bertram, who allow their four children to grow up with very little restraint or set programme of education, being thrown for the most part into the hands of their self-interested Aunt Norris. Only Fanny Price, totally neglected by her aunt, escapes such a fate, and is shown by Austen to be devout and engaged in a programme of self-teaching, emerging unscathed as a principled, informed and independent young lady, even able to refuse what seems to other minds an advantageous marriage proposal from someone whose character she can never respect and whom she could never love or trust. This is contrasted in *Agnes Grey* with the complete lack of information and total lack of self-restraint evident in Rosalie Murray, who accepts Sir Thomas Ashby with little thought of the future.

It is in *Emma* that we meet Austen's only governess – Miss Taylor/ Mrs. Weston, except for the potential governess, Jane Fairfax, who thankfully avoids such a fate. Mrs. Weston resembles Agnes Grey only in one small aspect. Mr. Knightley notes how she never succeeds in getting Emma to do more than draw up lists of good books to read but never undergoing 'any course of steady reading' (p. 602). This is like Agnes Grey who was considered unfit for her appointment with the Murrays and who also did not succeed in tutoring Rosalie or Matilda to attain 'such a complete education as [her] powers would seem to promise' (*Emma,* p.602). Both governesses certainly did their best to deal with the problems that the parents, through sheer indulgence of their children, had caused in the first place.

In *Persuasion,* we meet another father figure, Sir Walter Elliot, uninterested in his three daughters except for their personal appearance and how they can help his self-vanity. One can only assume that it is through the mother's good sense and that of her dear friend, Lady Russell, that the middle daughter, Anne Elliot, has managed to escape his attention and thereby to grow to resemble her mother rather than her father. Indeed, it is only in Anne that Lady Russell thinks 'that she could fancy the mother to revive again' (*Persuasion,* p.932), again like Agnes Grey, whose character Brontë portrays as greatly resembling that of her mother's.

Influence of Samuel Richardson

It remains uncertain whether Brontë was familiar with Samuel Richardson's works; yet once again, parallels between them can easily be established. As already noted in *Agnes Grey*, Brontë uses, as does Richardson, a first-person female narrator, whereas Jane Austen used instead third-person narrators. Later, in her second novel, Brontë uses multiple first-person narrators, starting with Gilbert

Markham's letter, followed by Helen's embedded narration in her secret diary and ending with Gilbert's letter.

Brontë's and Richardson's published aim of a moral focus to art, which should both instruct and entertain, can once again be seen to be remarkably similar to both authors. In *Agnes Grey,* Agnes aims to make 'Virtue practicable, Instruction desirable and Religion lovely and comprehensible (p.28), interlinking all three qualities strongly, as does Richardson too. Both authors seek to educate their public via the education of their heroines. '*Agnes Grey* is foremost a novel dealing with education; it is a novel *of* education (Agnes's) and *about* education (her attempts as governess to educate her charges) whose goal is to bring about an education in the reader'.[64] Brontë achieves this goal through her use of examples taken from the daily tutoring of her charges. On the very first page of *Agnes Grey*, Brontë talks of the 'treasure' of instruction, which is truth, stating rather modestly, that it will be for the reader to judge whether the content of her novel will prove useful or simply entertaining (p.15): 'All true histories contain instruction'. 'Whether this be the case with my history or not, I am hardly competent to judge. I sometimes think it might prove useful to some, and entertaining to others'. A comparison between Richardson's title page and his preface to *Pamela* and Brontë's first page of *Agnes Grey* and her *Preface to the Second Edition* of *The Tenant of Wildfell Hall*[65] reveals this startling similarity of aims. On the title page of *Pamela*, Richardson introduces the idea of publishing a book 'in order to cultivate the principles of virtue and religion in the minds of the youth of both sexes', a goal already stated as being dear to Brontë's heart. Indeed, Richardson's preface to *Pamela* claims requirements which could well be mistaken for Brontë's:

> 'If to divert and entertain, and at the same time to instruct and improve the minds of the youth of both sexes:
> If to inculcate religion and morality in so easy and agreeable a manner, as shall render them equally delightful and profitable:
> If to set forth in the most exemplary lights, the parental, the filial, and the social duties:
> If to paint vice in its proper colours, to make it deservedly odious; and to set virtue in its own amiable light, to make it look lovely.'

Brontë reiterates in her *Preface to the Second Edition* that her object in writing 'was not simply to amuse the Reader, neither was it to gratify [her] own taste', but rather because she 'wished to tell the truth, for truth always conveys its own moral to those who are able to receive it.' She relates, just as Richardson had done, why she has drawn her characters in such an honest fashion: 'when we have to do with vice and vicious characters, I maintain it is better to depict them as they really are than as they would wish to appear'. 'Is it better to reveal the snares and pitfalls of life to the young and thoughtless traveller, or to cover them with branches and flowers? Oh, Reader! if there were less of this delicate concealment of facts – this whispering 'Peace, peace,' when there is no peace, there would be less of sin and misery to the young of both sexes who are left to wring their bitter knowledge from experience.'

It is also uncertain whether Brontë read Richardson's sequel to *Pamela,* called *Pamela in her Exalted Condition (1741),* which, although it greatly involves the heroine's commentary on John Locke's *Some Thoughts concerning Education (1693),* has, as its predominant theme, pregnancy and child-rearing. *Pamela, Part 2,* as it is sometimes called, bears some similarities with Brontë's work in the sentiments which come out of the discussion between Mr. Locke and Mr. B.[66] Locke advocates a Stoic, physically inclined education for children, whom he feels should not be over-indulged. Certainly, in this aspect Brontë follows his suggestions. He is against corporal punishment, except when it really has to be administered, and then preferably by a tutor rather than a parent. This is not Anne Brontë's point of view, for she follows the more biblical approach of 'spare the rod and spoil the child'. Her governess, Agnes Grey, is depicted as wishing occasionally in desperation to be able to use a birch rod on Tom Bloomfield to punish him, especially in the episode of the birds' nest.

Locke advocates psychological rather than financial or material rewards for children's good behaviour, an idea followed by Brontë in *Agnes Grey,* where the Bloomfield children are given either cheerful or miserable compositions to prepare, dependent on their behaviour. Locke thoroughly approves of a mother taking a hand in educating her own children, as does Richardson's fictional heroine, Pamela, and Brontë follows him in this, for both her heroines, Agnes and Helen, gladly take on the responsibility for instructing their own children.

In Richardson's *Clarissa,* we see Clarissa disobey her family's wish to marry her to an older, degenerate man, Roger Solmes (whom she detests and whose character would never allow her to love, nor even to respect), and follow instead her attraction for the handsome, intelligent but feckless Robert Lovelace. This has some slight similarity with what happens to Helen Huntingdon in *The Tenant of Wildfell Hall,* for she too, in total disobedience to the wishes of her aunt, marries a most unsuitable man in preference to her aunt's choice of an older, but, in this case, more respectable suitor. Later, she relates in her diary how sorry she is that she wilfully went ahead in marrying such an unsuitable person without paying enough attention to the words of advice proffered by her aunt. Once more, we see evidence in literature of the erroneous conviction of the day that the love of a good woman could rescue a husband from a life of wickedness. Both heroines, the eighteenth-century Clarissa and the nineteenth-century Helen, are guilty of wilfulness and pride in thinking they are able to reform their suitors.

Influence of Magazines, Monthly Journals and Newspapers

Apart from eighteenth-century fiction, monthly journals such as *Blackwood's Magazine*, which the family read from 1817 to 1831, followed by *Fraser's Magazine* from 1831 on, also played their part in influencing Brontë's writing. In addition, she had access to a run of her late mother's *Methodist Magazines* from 1798 to 1812, which might well have furnished her with some religious source material for her novels. Charlotte in *Shirley, (p.389)* alludes to these magazines, calling them: 'Some mad, Methodist Magazines, full of miracles and apparitions of preternatural warnings, ominous dreams, and frenzied fanaticism'. These are attributed by Juliet Barker to Aunt Branwell, and could easily have been salvaged from the shipwreck of Anne's mother's belongings, along with some other Lady's Magazines.

In addition, newspapers proved invaluable in filling in some of the gaps in her knowledge of parental and marital relationships. The much publicized marriage and continuing romance of Queen Victoria and Prince Albert, no doubt, cheered her and the whole nation, but many other cases of less successful marriages also appeared in the press. One which hit the headlines in 1836, the year before Victoria's accession to the throne and when Brontë was just 16 years of age, was that of Caroline Norton, wife of George Norton, who was charged with 'Criminal Conversation', a euphemism for adultery, for receiving unchaperoned visits from the Prime-Minister, Lord Melbourne. Caroline was subsequently denied access to her child and was ostracized by society. In the penurious state in which she was left she had no alternative but to earn her living by the only legitimate means left open to her, her artistic talent. An initial example of earning money by selling paintings is mentioned early on in *Agnes Grey*, where Agnes's sister, Mary Grey, successfully raises enough money for her father's convalescence by selling off her water-colours. Brontë then goes on to use the better known example of Helen, after her flight, selling her paintings in order to support her son, servant and herself. This means of earning a living for well-educated females in desperate straits was evidently not unknown in the nineteenth century, as revealed by the oil painting of 1857, *Nameless and Friendless,* by Emily Mary Osborn.[67] This vividly portrays a young lady, accompanied by a young boy, who could well be her son, presenting her painting for sale. She is a Romanticized figure with a Madonna-like expression, who stands helplessly, clothed in a hooded cape, before the would-be buyer. Both her expression and the position of her hands indicate her apprehension as to how the transaction will turn out, as she and her son look anxiously towards the gentleman examining the painting.

Helen's hurried departure from the financial security of her husband's home had to be carried out in the utmost secrecy, for the position of wives in such situations, in the early nineteenth century, was most precarious. Once married, the wife and her possessions belonged to the husband; she and her children could then be treated as his chattels without any intervention by the law. The wife was unable to leave her husband's home of her own accord as, if found, she could easily have been imprisoned at his instigation for her 'crime'. Brontë was well aware that there was no possibility of divorce for married women in such circumstances, for the Matrimonial Causes Act was not introduced until 1857 and the Property Act for Married Women did not come in until 1870-72. Unless there were incest or bigamy, no divorce bill, presented on a woman's behalf, had any chance of success even as late as 1848, when *The Tenant* was published. One such Bill was introduced by a lady of influential family, who claimed that her husband had been unfaithful to her on their wedding night, had seduced all the female servants in the house, had transmitted venereal disease to herself and was constantly drunk. Yet, although it was also known at the time this Bill was put forward that her husband was a prisoner of the King's Bench and being kept there in comfort by the earnings of a prostitute, it still failed to be passed in her favour. It was not until 1857 that actions for 'criminal conversation', as in Caroline Norton's case, were abolished[68] and women had to wait until 1923 to gain equality of access to divorce on the grounds of a husband's infidelity. Brontë, as aware as she could be for her times, did not attempt to present a political case for change in such unfavourable circumstances, but rather attempted a psychological study of such effects upon women, which she wrote as a means of alerting them to avoid making such mistaken choices in future. Helen Huntingdon had been compelled to close her door on her husband and also to flee from him, although she was fully aware that, if she had been caught, she could easily have been imprisoned with all access to her child utterly denied her, as indeed happened to Caroline Norton, who, once separated from her husband, was allowed no further contact with her infant. Brontë felt strongly about such inequality of the sexes which she saw all around her, but, as a visionary for the future, her real anxieties extended to the educational methods adopted by parents towards their children. Yet, although visionary, she was still realistic enough in her approach to show her interest in offering solutions in her novels which could help to eradicate those ills from society with even more immediacy of effect than the passing of laws or reform bills.

Chapter Six:

Critical reception of Brontë's novels by her contemporaries

Brontë's views, as expressed in her novels, did not always meet with the approval of her day. Her greatest critic was, indeed, her sister, Charlotte, which must have caused her a lot of pain as can be seen from the poem she wrote on 24 April 1848, whilst deeply engrossed in the writing of *The Tenant*:

> 'Believe not those who say
> The upward path is smooth,
>
> Arm, arm thee for the fight!
> Toil through the hottest day.
>
> Crush pride into the dust,
> See not they treasure here;
>
> What matters who should whisper blame,
> Or who should scorn or slight?
>
> What matters – if thy God approve,
> And if within thy breast,
> Thou feel the comfort of his love,
> The earnest of his rest.[69]

Charlotte disapproved of Anne's second novel for, after her younger sister's death, she expressed her distaste for its subject in the Biographical Notice of Ellis and Acton Bell, which she wrote in 1850 for the reprint of *Agnes Grey* and *Wuthering Heights*, saying, *'The Tenant of Wildfell Hall* by Acton Bell, had likewise an unfavourable reception. At this I cannot wonder. The choice of subject was an entire mistake' (AG p.8). Charlotte does not stop there, although she understood perfectly (as is evident from her 1850 preface to the reprint of *Agnes Grey* and *The Tenant of Wildfell Hall),* the motivation which drove the reserved Anne Brontë to lay her experience and deepest thoughts before the public gaze. She failed miserably to credit her youngest sister's subject with any taste or power. Instead, Charlotte treated Anne's second novel, *The Tenant*, as a foible of the baby of the family, who, contrary to her eldest sister's advice, refused to listen to reason and change her distasteful choice of subject.[70] As a result, it was not just *The Tenant* which fell into a seemingly deliberately engendered period of oblivion, but also *Agnes Grey*, which was not given the prominence it deserved as the first of its genre to use the subject of a plain governess to succeed in finding marital happiness. Anne's first novel was termed imitative of Charlotte's *Jane Eyre*, when, in actual effect, it preceded her sister's work by several months, breaking new ground entirely, with its unassuming, ordinary heroine.[71] She goes on to spell out the motives of her youngest sister as being 'slightly morbid'. She blames Anne's contemplation of the terrible effects of talents misused and faculties abused; evidently thinking of Patrick Branwell, her brother, for her choice of subject. Charlotte mentions Anne's 'sensitive, reserved, and dejected nature;' and how Anne 'brooded over it till she believed it to be a duty to reproduce every detail (of course with fictitious characters, incidents, and situation) as a warning to others'. Indeed, Flora Katherine Willett supports the view that 'Charlotte's underestimation of Anne is not only grossly inaccurate but also legend'.[72] Charlotte also admits to have reasoned with Anne, trying to change her mind for she says: 'When reasoned with on the subject, she regarded such reasonings as a temptation to self-indulgence. She must be honest, she must not varnish, soften, or conceal.' (Biographical Notice, pp.8/9) In addition, she mentions that Anne was 'a very sincere and practical Christian', who suffered from 'a tinge of religious melancholy' which cast a shadow on her 'sad, blameless life'. This is dismissive, to say the least, of Anne's ability to think for herself. Charlotte is evidently annoyed that Anne went ahead with the publishing of this subject, which reveals all the unsavoury details of life at the Parsonage over the last few years that perhaps Charlotte had not wanted divulged. Charlotte had been the one to wash her hands of her brother in these last days and certainly did not want Anne to drag this morbid subject into the public gaze and in so doing possibly tarnish her own and her sister's reputations. In any case, Charlotte did her best to keep *The Tenant* out of public view for about a decade. Was her motive pure, or was it simply done out of snobbery and annoyance at Anne's stepping outside the boundaries of convention and thereby laying Charlotte open to being labelled by some of the critics with the same coarseness and brutality that Anne had had to endure? After all, *The Spectator* said in an unsigned review on 3 July, 1848: 'there seems in the writer a morbid love for the coarse not to say the brutal' 'there is a coarseness of tone throughout the writing of all these Bells'. Dr. Robert Barnard supports the idea of snobbery associated with the Brontës in his statement that *Blackwood's Magazine,* which they all read avidly, encouraged 'the unattractive mixture of social and intellectual snobbery in the young Brontës' hearts'. He also reveals that Charlotte felt that Dickens wrote on 'low' subjects and apparently supported Thackeray's statement that Dickens was 'embarrassingly coarse, vulgar and happy'.[73] Indeed, society at the time, according to Charlotte's letter to Ellen Nussey in July 1842,[74] reacted against Dicken's 'low' subjects. So, was Charlotte's dislike of Anne's disclosure of their private circumstances and her attack on the upper classes' attitude to marriage and parenting, motivated by snobbery or by the social climate which Charlotte felt Anne had portrayed in her second novel? A further point to consider is Charlotte's attitude towards the Whites, who employed her as governess. It is more than evident that she feels a certain snootiness towards them, considering them as quite vulgar tradespeople. Lady Wilson also comments on Charlotte's 'distaste for . . . any morbid exhibitions of emotion.'[75] implying that Charlotte might well have resented, as the private person she was, Anne's exhibiting to a large reading public the personal details of her family's tragedy. One must also consider that Charlotte might have been a little jealous of Anne, whose *Tenant,* was accepted for publication before her *The Professor*, and although it received some unfavourable criticism, did indeed sell well and was already into its second reprint within a month of first issue date; hence Anne's preface of 1848. Yet, that argument does not bear much weight, as Charlotte's *Jane Eyre* was itself a tremendous success and was supported by such writers as Swinburne, who admired Charlotte's and Emily's work, but found *The Tenant* 'ludicrously weak, palpably unreal and apparently imitative ' (of Jane Eyre). One wonders what novel he was reading in attributing such an adjective as *'unreal'* to *The Tenant.* Evidently, he did not realise that Anne was the first to introduce a plain governess.[76]

More important perhaps to Charlotte, was the fact that Anne had succeeded as a governess, whereas she had not, and had attained a high emolument of £10 a quarter or £40 yearly with the Robinson's, whereas Charlotte's post with the Whites of Rawdon, trades people as opposed to landed gentry, had brought in only half this amount. To her friend, Ellen Nussey, Charlotte writes on 5 February 1850, that *The Tenant of Wildfell Hall* 'hardly appears to me desirable to preserve'. Here the voice of authority of the eldest sister speaks. Yet, against all this, Charlotte continually gave signs to Ellen of her great affection for her younger sister, saying that Anne's subject was 'too little consonant with the character – tastes and ideas of the gentle, retiring, inexperienced writer', which suggests a concern on

Charlotte's behalf of her sister Anne's 'religious melancholy'. Charlotte substantiates this religious issue even further by saying that amongst Anne's papers she found 'mournful proofs that that was the case.' She forgets, perhaps deliberately, that, while she was at Roe Head School, she too had been seriously depressed spiritually by her worries over the Calvinistic faith, which she often discussed in her letters to Ellen.

Apart from what Charlotte said about Anne's writings, let us look more closely at what the critics were saying about Anne's second novel. George Moore, after his extensive praise of *Agnes Grey* as 'the most perfect prose narrative in English Letters' *(Conversations in Ebury St, 1924),* recognised that Charlotte seemed to be deliberately trying to depreciate Anne's work after her death. He saw in Anne 'a quality of heat' which might, even in ten years or so, have given her a place beside or higher than Jane Austen.[77] Sharpe's *London Magazine,* however, warned its female readers not to read her work, noting its 'profane expressions, inconceivably coarse language, and revolting scenes and descriptions by which its pages are disfigured' (Unsigned review, August 1848). *The Rambler* said that *The Tenant* had the same faults as *Jane Eyre,* which they thought was 'one of the coarsest books which we ever perused' (Again an unsigned review, September 1848).

Still, these are not the questions to be resolved here, for the fact remains, that whether many of her contemporary critics hated the coarseness of her subject matter or not, none of them asked the question what Brontë was attempting to reveal in her novels, coarse or not, nor did they comprehend the intensity of her sentiments, nor her need to make them public. The reasons behind Anne's voluntary relinquishing of her privacy to concentrate, during the last years of her life, on the experiences she had lived through, are clearly set out by her in her *Preface.* She selflessly overcomes her reticence to speak in order to warn her generation, and those to come, of the dangers of continuing with the same attitudes towards the lack of education of women, class distinction, marriages of convenience and bad parenting. Unflinchingly, she gives everything that is important to her over to the public, relaying her experiences to her readers to help them to live, in the future, by more Godly principles. As she tells us in her poem, *Believe not those who say* (24 April 1848), she was prepared to stand the tiredness, the toil, the pride and the whispered blame, just to make the public aware of how some could be saved from mistakes like those which had affected her brother and those her employers had made towards their children. She emphasised certain guide-lines by which it would be possible for parents and children to achieve happy relationships and to live together a life of mutual respect and love, instead of one of the misery, which she witnessed daily around her.

Anne's thoughts resemble those of one of her contemporaries, Sarah Lewis, who was writing in *Woman's Mission* in 1840 on the standards of education necessary to change the tenor of social morality and help to bring about greater love and better relationships between parents and children. Sarah says: 'Let every woman then engrave upon the heart of her son such an image of feminine virtue and loveliness, as may make it sufficient for him to turn his eyes inward to draw then a power sufficient to combat evil and to preserve him from wretchedness'.[78] In the same way as Sarah's advice should be taken seriously, Anne's advocating the need to seek after loving family relationships and to live by a strong code of ethics should also be viewed in this light, for, if followed, it could well be the means of revolutionizing a change in the attitude of our present generation, as Anne had so desired for hers. It could even help to arrest the ever-growing numbers of unwanted and unloved children, products of the numerous split marriages of our times. Her warning, which speaks loudly and clearly to all parents, including the single mothers of today, and to whole generations of fatherless children, would do well to be heeded.

Conclusion

Anne Brontë, aware of the injustice of her age especially as regards the lack of equal opportunities for men and women, determined, as a devout Christian, to tackle such issues in her two novels, which would bear her pseudonym of Acton Bell and thereby shield her from the prejudice of the day of being known as a woman writer. Her Evangelical approach to writing emphasized the importance of living by a strong code of ethics and at the same time diffused, especially in her second novel, her confused views on Universal Salvation, which she felt would offer some hope of eternal life not only to herself and to those dear to her but also to her readers. Her age demanded that she write a literature 'which was not primarily for entertainment or aesthetic gratification but for its effects on man's moral and social consciousness'[79] which suited her very well. She was insistent on adding an entertainment factor to her novels to ensure that the public might thereby be enticed to read her work and absorb her teaching indirectly. Her message in *Agnes Grey* is directed at any unmarried female who might need to earn a living, especially as a governess, and is one of encouragement and guidance in the face of the great oppression and inequality of opportunities existing in her age. Marriage is shown by her to be a blessing only if it is entered upon with self-control and caution and based on a mutual love or respect. Advice is offered too for those married ladies who, like Rosalie Murray/Lady Ashby, have taken the fatal step lightly and inadvisedly through ignorance and lack of parental guidance. Her message in *The Tenant of Wildfell Hall* is directed primarily at any 'rash youth' or 'thoughtless girl' to prevent them both from following in the footsteps of either her unhappy scapegrace, Huntingdon, or 'from falling into the very natural error' of her heroine, Helen.[80]

Her novels are not overtly didactic for her practical advice is cleverly concealed in her illustrations, many of which are amusing accounts taken from real life, where she juxtaposes both sides of her argument so that the reader, provided with the full picture, can make up his own mind. Evidently, her hope is that by not proffering prescriptive guide-lines those members of society, already arrogant and rebellious enough, would still be attracted to her writings and be influenced by them. Her initial critical reception did not support this hope of hers. Her caring love for her pupils is seen depicted in her fictional heroine, Agnes, where even her silence speaks volumes. When Agnes is confronted by malicious teasing from Rosalie Murray, who is trying to captivate Mr. Weston to relieve her boredom and also to make her governess aware of her superior attractions, Agnes prefers to remain silent. Lines from Anne's poem, *Fragment*:[81]

> 'Yes I will take a cheerful tone
> And feign to share their heartless glee,
> But I would rather weep alone
> Than laugh amid their revelry'

show how often she had been subjected to such treatment and had had to use self-control to refrain from rebuking her opponents, and explains in part why Agnes also prefers to remain silent on many occasions rather than retaliate. Anne intelligently calculates her readers' response to such illustrations as these, which she uses to help those who are young enough to be re-educated and thereby saved from a life of wretchedness, of which Anne had living proof at the Parsonage. The indulgence shown to Branwell had led him to the state of lack of self-control in which he had been since his dismissal from Thorp Green in July 1845. Anne had daily witnessed his descent into stupor and was desperate to promote her message of hope to those who might listen and, consequently, be saved in the future from such suffering. Since 1843, when Branwell had, at her instigation, started work at the Robinsons' home as a tutor to Edmund Robinson, Anne had had to witness in silence the adulterous relationship which was forming between himself and her employer's wife:

> 'Grieving to look on vice and sin
> yet powerless to quell,
> the silent current from within,
> the outward torrent's swell'

> While all the good I would impart,
> turned to wormwood there'.[82]

Evidently by May 1845, Anne, conscious of what was happening at Thorp Green, passionately felt the need to impart good. As mentioned, in her own diary entry of 31 July 1845, Anne wrote 'during my stay I have had some very unpleasant and undreamt of experience of human nature', and in the back of her Common Prayer book she wrote, 'Sick of mankind and their disgusting ways'.

Indeed, her novels advocate the cultivation of certain qualities in her characters which Anne maintains will, if striven for and attained, bring about as much earthly happiness as possible and more importantly help lead to the reward of eternal life. These qualities are revealed in her fictional heroes and heroines such as Agnes Grey, Mr. Weston, and even in the less perfect Gilbert Markham. Agnes is seen to be devout, humble, modest, forgiving, patient, caring and, above all, very self-controlled. Mr. Weston too is devout, humble, non-boastful, solid, decent and a cautious individual, who examines Agnes carefully before committing himself to her as a future marriage partner. These qualities greatly resemble those listed by Hannah More in her *Moral Sketches of Prevailing Opinions and Manners*. The qualities suggested by More are 'solid judgment, heroic fortitude, Christian humility, unshaken trust in God and submission to his dispensation', all of which are compatible with Anne's choice. What is more, they are diametrically opposed to the faults she depicts in Arthur Huntingdon and his merry band of 'profligate companions'.[83] Such characters and their foils are used by Anne to allow her readers to assess for themselves from the illustrations given, rather than be issued with direct instructions as to how to proceed in life.

Anne expresses very clear views on the marriages of convenience of her day as in the cases of Rosalie Murray/ Lady Ashby, and Milicent Hargrave/ Mrs. Hatfield. These examples are clearly portrayed by her as unhappy unions, where money and status are considered by the parents as the only necessary requirements for the marriage. Indeed, this attitude often featured in Victorian times where the gentry tried to promote wealth amongst themselves by the inter-marrying of their sons and daughters, in order to achieve maximum wealth and status for them both. Anne offers hope to women who have made such a rash step and her advice is certainly not just targeted at the single woman like herself, who, in the future, might have to make up her mind about marriage, but also at any married lady who, having 'made her bed, is now having to lie on it'. The young Lady Ashby, despairing over the lack of change in the behaviour of her husband, is just such an example. She is given simple, clear advice by her former governess and current friend, Agnes, who tells her 'first, by gentle reasoning, by kindness, example, and persuasion to try and ameliorate her husband, and then when she had done all she could, if she still found him incorrigible, to endeavour to abstract herself from him – to wrap herself up in her own integrity and trouble herself as little about him as possible' (A.G. p.282). In Anne's second novel, Helen Huntingdon actually carries out this advice, doing her best to live as happily as she can under horrendous circumstances. Anne, via Agnes, advises any married lady living in such miserable circumstances 'to seek consolation in doing her duty to God and man, to put her trust in Heaven, and solace herself with the care and nurture of her little daughter' (AG, p.282). She aims at revealing, through the unhappiness of such unions, that, for those who intend to marry, there is a better way of making the marital choice. She urges her readers (not directly but through her characters' experiences) to search for compatibility, mutual love and respect rather than just money, leading us to believe through her illustrations of marriages that do work, that this is indeed the only way to approach the whole question. She gives examples of a multitude of successful marriages including those of Agnes's parents; of Agnes's own with Mr. Weston (who, showing his usual caution, confirms that he will be able to maintain a wife on his stipend of £300 a year); of her friend Milicent, in the latter stages of her marriage to the reformed Hatfield; of Helen's second marriage to Gilbert Markham; of Rose Markham's marriage to Halford; of Mary Millward's marriage to Richard Wilson; of Lord Lowborough's second marriage; and of Helen's own brother's marriage to Esther Hargrave. The list is endless and the examples are legion, all testifying to the fact that marriage is sanctified by God and should only be undertaken when both parties are mutually attracted and hold similar principles.

The focus of her novels could be considered to be relatively narrow, for her advice is directed more at the educated, both at the wealthy gentry of her age and at those brought up in middle-class households like her own. Granted, she does reveal a charitable spirit in her novel to help the poor like Nancy Brown but her greatest concern remains with the education of women like herself. To be fair, her proximity to landed gentry, which extended over most of her adult life, especially the five years of her post as governess to the Robinsons, would have pushed her in that direction. From the age of nineteen years to twenty-five years, her role was to educate the children of the rich and influential members of Victorian society, where undoubtedly she would have witnessed, at first hand, the arrogance and snobbery of class distinction, imposed on such as herself, a mere paid employee, who was engaged simply to conform to the fashion and requirements of the wealthy to have a governess for their children. Another factor, which did not help to position governesses clearly in society, was, as already mentioned, the way in which their employers acted towards them. Governesses, indeed, had to be more than endowed with Christian qualities of patience, strength and forbearance in Anne Brontë's day, to survive the ordeals of rejection to which they were undoubtedly subjected.

In targeting amongst all women the many spinsters, like herself, well-educated and without a dowry, who, in the climate of the day where too many women existed for too few men, had very little chance of finding a husband, Anne encourages them never to 'shrink from the work that God has set before [them], because it was not fitted to [their] taste?' (AG p.263). She looked at the facts and realistically assessed that, like herself, they had to earn a living in order to survive or to help their families financially. Indeed, in *Agnes Grey,* when all hope of marriage seems distant and Mr. Weston has, so far, failed to make an appearance, as Agnes had hoped, after much soul-searching, she simply persists in working hard. She decides that, with God's help, the best way forward is for her to address herself diligently to her appointed duty and 'endeavour to promote the welfare of those around [her] (p.263)' looking to the hereafter for her reward.

According to Lord Morris the late President of the Brontë Society, the 1851 Census showed that there were 24,270 governesses registered. Mary Taylor, one of Charlotte's best friends, however, was quite adamant that she would not join this profession and preferred to leave England, as did many other young ladies for North Island, New Zealand, stating that she would most certainly 'not be a governess, a teacher, a milliner, a bonnet-maker nor housemaid. She sees no means of obtaining employment she would like in England, so she is leaving it.' (CB to EJB, 2 April, 1841).[84] The choice of jobs for women was indeed limited in Anne Brontë's day and she cannot have been unaware of the oppression of women in a society where, although there were fewer men, there existed most certainly much male domination. Betty Jay[85] is convinced that Anne Brontë knew about the many Governess debates of the 1840s which elaborated on the power struggles encountered by the educated middle-class women forced to take on paid work and consequently subjected to a lack of respect from both employers and society at large. Through her fictional character, Helen Huntingdon, Brontë guides women subjected, as was Helen, to callous cruelty, mental and sometimes physical, giving a real-life example of her own experience of witnessing such lives of misery from behind the closed doors of both Victorian gentry and middle-class households.

Brontë's overcoming of her innate shyness and her fearlessness in speaking out evidently arises from seeing about her such hopelessness in terms of marital and parental relationships. Her novels were written to help people cope with such injustices, but not from a subversive feminist point of view like that of Mary Wollstonecraft, who spoke out against the sanctity of marriage and property laws, nor from that of Lady Morgan in an attempt 'to disgrace man'.[86] She was not interested in putting forward a political point of view in favour of equal rights before the law for men and women, although she was very conscious of the great ills of her age. She was more engrossed in the reality of the situation as it existed, and in presenting solutions through her guide-lines, so that problems could be attenuated. Nor did she accept the ideology of her age which encouraged women to make use of their supposed spiritual superiority over men within their domestic sphere and their presumed redemptory positions.

Brontë states through her fictional characters that woman should not be ignorant of the world and should be educated and independent enough to make an informed choice of either marriage partner or job. This is again very like Hannah More's attitude, for the latter insists on a young woman being 'well-informed', who should not 'push herself to use her knowledge to exercise power. She must be able to join in the conversation when required, but to leave leadership to men'.[87] Even Caroline Norton, whose husband brought a case for divorce against Lord Melbourne, declared in 1838 that 'the natural position of women is inferiority to men . . . Amen! . . . the wild and stupid theories advanced by a few women of 'equal rights' and 'equal intelligence' are not the opinion of their sex.'[88] Brontë's fictional characters are not portrayed as merely struggling to find independence from the dominance of men, but more as feminine creatures, who do not seek to be oppressed, but who, as long as mutual love, respect and trust exist in the relationship, rather enjoy the man in their life taking charge. It is certainly not Anne's desire to belittle men to further the cause of women. Helen is not portrayed by her as fleeing Huntingdon's household so as to advocate that way forward for every unhappy wife but rather to suggest caution, great reflection and a greater knowledge of the world as necessary to prevent a young woman from getting involved in a similarly incompatible union to Helen's. As Anne herself says, she is not introducing such a character as 'a specimen' of the common practices of society, for the case given is an extreme one, but she continues by adding that she knows 'such characters do exist,' and that if she can prevent anyone from walking that path she will not have written her book in vain. Anne upholds the sanctity of matrimony and is intent on promoting better marital relationships in order to produce better parents and thereby to change society from its roots. Had she not witnessed in her second post as governess the effect that Mrs. Robinson's misguided actions had on her three daughters who, although they continued to love their governess after she left their home, even coming to see her at Haworth Parsonage, unfortunately through the lack of guidance received from their parents, especially from their mother, caused scandal in their own marriages?

From 1830 on, in the post-Romantic period, the realistic novel dominated rather than poetry, as had been previously the case. Anne Brontë used the art form of her novels to give her perception of the world to her public, so granting them insight into the way ordinary people thought and acted in her generation. She put her imagination and experience to work and told stories which engaged the attention of her public, creating enough excitement to keep her readers interested. She concentrated on giving a picture of the world which was to shape the change she so desired, and thereby distinguished herself as the author of great realistic novels, written to reflect ordinary life and to change people's lives. Lewes, George Eliot's common law partner,[89] said it was more complicated to imagine the ordinary life than the fantastic and this is just what Anne Brontë does in both her novels. She sets aside her own desire for privacy and through her own personal sufferings in seeing her brother brought so low understands what it is like to be someone else, identifying herself strongly with her two fictional characters, Agnes and Helen, so that there can be remoulding of the lives of her readers, who are also encouraged to identify with them and learn from their experiences. Anne's novels help us to penetrate more deeply into ordinary human life and increase our realization of the oppression of women in Victorian homes and of the terrible lack of women's education in her generation which could have enabled them to cope more readily with marriage and the rearing of children. She allows us through her characters' dialogue to hear what is going on in other people's minds and encourages us through her many illustrations to relate to the characters and so to absorb the goodness of her advice.

The theme of parenting, discussed at length in this book, emerges as one of the most important of the topics that Anne discusses and evidently, although some of her contemporaries reacted badly to her novel with a purpose as lurid sensationalism, some did listen to her message. Literature was used by Brontë to make her readers think seriously about reforming their ways and her strong advice on how to set about educating men and women to be able to make informed choices as regards marriage, work and the upbringing of children was not always acceptable or immensely popular in her age. As in Elizabeth Gaskell's *Mary Barton* or *Ruth,* both of which also attracted criticism, some reforming of ways did come about as a result of the strength of her appeal. Her courage allowed her to proceed and, although the reading public was thwarted by her early death, and her sister's denigration of the subject of *The Tenant,* much more attention is now beginning to be focused on this much neglected writer who parented her two novels as lovingly and conscientiously as if they had been her own children.

Selected Bibliography

A Kempis, Thomas, *Of the Imitation of Christ,* ed. Rivington, London.
Austen, Jane, *The Complete Novels,* BCA, Crown Publishers, Kent, 1999.
Barker, Dr. Juliet, *The Brontës,* Orion Books Ltd., Phoenix, 1995.
The Brontës. A Life in Letters, Penguin Group, England, 1997.
Bellamy, Joan, *More Precious than Rubies,* Highgate Publications, 2002.
Bible, N.I.V., Hodder & Stoughton, 1998.
Brontë, Anne, *Agnes Grey,* ed. Temple Scott, John Grant, Edinburgh, 1911.
The Tenant of Wildfell Hall, edited by G. D. Hargreaves, Penguin Classics, 1985.
Preface to the Second Edition of the *Tenant,* 22 July, 1848.
Brontë, Charlotte, *Biographical Notice of Ellis and Acton Bell, 19 Sept. 1850.*
The Professor, edited by Heather Glen, Penguin Classics, 1989.
Brunton, Mary, *Discipline,* Pandora Press, London, 1986.
Chaber, Dr. Lois A., '*Mr. Locke and Mr. B.',* Part 2 of *Pamela,* in *Studies in eighteenth-century Culture,* Volume 18, American Society for eighteenth-century Studies.
Chitham, Dr. Edward, *The Poems of Anne Brontë,* Macmillan, 1979.
A Life of Anne Brontë, Blackwell, Oxford, 1997.
Davies, Dr. Stevie, *The Pilgrimage of Anne Brontë,* B.S.T., April 2000.
Gaskell, Elizabeth C., *Wives and Daughters,* Penguin, 1999.
Ruth, edited by Angus Easson, Penguin, 1997.
Life of Charlotte Brontë, edited by Alan Shelston, Penguin, 1975
Gérin, Winifred, *Anne Brontë,* Thomas Nelson & Sons, London, 1959.
Branwell Brontë, Nelson & Sons, 1961.
Introduction to *The Tenant of Wildfell Hall,* Penguin Classics, 1985.
Higuchi, Akiko, *Anne Brontë's Song Book* and *Branwell Brontë's Flute Book,* foreword by Bob Duckett, 2002.
Jay, Betty, *Anne Brontë,* Writers & their work, Northcote House, Tavistock, 2000.
Langland, Elizabeth, *Anne Brontë: the other one,* Barnes & Noble, 1989.
Moore, Jane, *Mary Wollstonecraft,* Writers & their work, Plymouth, 1999.
More, Hannah, *Coelebs in search of a wife,* edited by Mary Waldron, Thoemmes Press, 1995.
New Approaches to the Literary Art of Anne Brontë, edited by Julie Nash and Barbara A. Suess, Ashgate, 2001.
Richardson, Samuel, *Pamela,* edited by Peter Sabor, Penguin, 1980.
Clarissa, Penguin Classics, 1985.
Social Contract, Essays by Locke, Hume and Rousseau, intro. by Sir Ernest Barker, (O.U.P., London).
Todd, Dr. Janet, *Mary Wollstonecraft: A Revolutionary Life,* (Columbia U.P. 1987). Also, *The Works of Mary Wollstonecraft,* edited by Janet Todd and Marilyn Butler, (Pickering and Chatto, 1989).
Tomalin, Claire, *The Life and Death of Mary Wollstonecraft,* Weidenfeld & Nicholson, 1995.
Waldron, Dr. Mary, *Jane Austen & the fiction of her time,* C.U.P., 1999.
Winnifrith, Dr. Tom, *The Brontës and their background,* Blackwell Ltd, Oxford, 1983.
The Poems of Patrick Branwell Brontë, edited by Tom Winnifrith.
Wollstonecraft, Mary, *Mary and the Wrongs of Woman,* The World's Classics, edited by Gary Kelly, O.U.P., Oxford, New York, 1988.
Yonge, Charlotte M., *The Clever Woman of the Family,* edited by Clare A. Simmons, Broadview Press, Canada, 2001.

Footnotes

1   Anne Brontë, *Agnes Grey,* edited by Temple Scott, (John Grant, Edinburgh, 1911*),
     Introduction* by Winifred Gérin.
2   Labelled as 'dear gentle Anne' by Ellen Nussey, as 'little, sweet, resigned, gentle,
     pious, delicate and passive' by her sister Charlotte, (who often exhibits a singular
     lack of understanding of her youngest sister), and as a 'gentle, quiet, rather
     subdued person' by George Smith, (Cornhill Magazine, December 1900). Anne,
     nevertheless, did not lack determination and excelled at concealing her feelings.
3   Charlotte Brontë, 'Biographical Notice of Ellis and Acton Bell, 19 September, 1850',
     (*Agnes Grey,* edited by Temple Scott), p.9.
4   Mary Waldron, *Jane Austen and the Fiction of her time,* (Cambridge University
     Press, 1999), p.119.
5   C. M. Yonge, *The Clever Woman of the Family,* ed. by Clare A. Simmons, (Broadview
     Press, 2001), p.547.
6   Branwell was undoubtedly present at the Parsonage in February 1836 as he was
     appointed to the Three Graces Masonic Lodge there and apparently never missed a
     monthly meeting throughout 1836 and 1837. Whether or not he went to London is
     unclear, but Emily, as we see from her Diary Paper of 26 June 1837, where she
     mentions her and Anne's Gondal involvement, also alludes to Branwell's Angrian
     scenes showing that she and Anne were perfectly au fait with Charlotte's and
     Branwell's literary compositions. See 'Anne Brontë's Religion. First signs of a
     breakdown in relations with Emily', by Mary Summers, *B.S.T.,* Vol.25, Pt.1, April
     2000.
7   This poem about the death of his beloved sister, Maria, reveals Branwell's fixation
     with regarding himself as one of the damned from as early as 2 March 1836. In this
     poem, *Misery. Part II,* he voices his doubts in no mean fashion. *Poems of Patrick
     Branwell Brontë,* ed. by Tom Winnifrith, (Blackwell Ltd, 1983), p.30.
8   This is recounted by Jane Moore in her biography of *Mary Wollstonecraft,* p.29.
9   Sally Hesketh, 'Needlework in the Lives and Novels of the Brontë Sisters', (*Brontë
     Society Transactions,* 1997), Vol. 22, p.78.
10   Mary Summers, *Eugénie de Guérin: A Life of Reaction,* (Edwin Mellen Press, 1997)
     available in soft-back from Le Musée-Château du Cayla, 81140 Andillac.
     S.W.France.
11   *Classics of Brontë Scholarship,* edited by Charles Lemmon, (*B.S.T.,* 1999), p.106.
12   There was quite a widespread Romantic Revival in English Literature in 1818,
     which influenced all forms of art including the Gondal tales, and also Brontë's
     endings of her novels.
13   Stevie Davies, 'The Pilgrimage of Anne Brontë', *(BST,* April 2000*),* p.12.
14   Charlotte Brontë, 'Biographical Notice of Ellis and Acton Bell, 19 September, 1850',
     (*Agnes Grey,* edited by Temple Scott), originally published by Smith, Elder and Co.
     for the reprint of *Wuthering Heights* and *Agnes Grey,* In 1850, Charlotte shows how
     difficult she found it to accept her sister's reasoning in defence of her second novel.
     Charlotte said of the matter: *'The choice of subject was an entire mistake . . . She
     brooded over it till she believed it to be a duty to reproduce every detail (of course with
     fictitious characters, incidents, and situations) as a warning to others' (p.8).*

15   Quotation taken from the Bible, Matt. 5 v.26 and cited by Helen in TWH, p.192.
16   Dr. Juliet Barker, *The Brontës*, (Phoenix, 1995), recounts the rumour spread by
      Nancy Garrs that 'the gardener employed by the Robinsons had surprised Branwell
      and Mrs. Robinson together in the boathouse at Scarborough and had informed the
      lady's husband. The gardener was identified as Robert Pottage, who, along with his
      wife, worked for the family'.
17   Maria Branwell Brontë died 21st September 1821, barely 20 months after Anne was
      born.
18   Elizabeth Langland, *Anne Brontë: the other one*, (Barnes and Noble, 1989) p.6.
19   Anne Brontë became both physically and spiritually ill some time before her return
      to Roe Head after the Christmas Holidays of 1837, for in Jan. 1838, she received a
      visit from a Moravian minister, James La Trobe. As yet, there is no record found of
      Anne's having visited Wellhouse, the Moravian Chapel at Mirfield.
20   Ellen Nussey commented on this to Charlotte. She describes their world as 'one of
      zestful cheerfulness and unchallenged independence.'
21   Tom Winnifrith, *The Brontës and their Background*, (Blackwell Ltd., 1983), p.54.
22   Winifred Gérin, *Branwell Brontë*, (Nelson & Sons, 1961, p.118). See also '*The Poems
      of Patrick Branwell Brontë*, edited by Tom Winnifrith, (Blackwell Ltd., 1983).
23   'The North Wind', in Edward Chitham's, *The Poems of Anne Brontë* (Macmillan,
      1979), p.63. Anne drew three sketches of a curly-haired baby in 1837, the last one
      finished just prior to the visit of La Trobe. The babies have large protuberant eyes
      and are not portrayed in her usual Romantic style and may well reflect her
      depressed state at the time. (See Illustrations 3 and 4).
24   See 'Despondency', written 20 December 1841, Chitham, p. 80.
25   Brontë was indeed stepping out in faith when she revealed her ideas on Universal
      Salvation and was a precursor of the Universalist theory of Salvation. Brontë's
      personal doctrine challenges the belief in eternal punishment current in the Church
      of England and indeed in most religious sects of the nineteenth century. Four years
      after her death, such views as hers were more widely known, for F. D. Maurice was
      deprived of his professorship at King's College, London, for proclaiming a belief in
      everlasting damnation. In his *Theological Essays* (1853), he argued that to believe
      that future punishment would be endless was a superstition. See A. N. Wilson, *The
      Victorians*, (2002), p.170. In 1877, Dean Farrar also went so far as to suggest in
      Eternal Hope, that salvation was for everyone.
26   'A Word to the Calvinists', No. 22, Chitham, p. 89.
27   'The Brontës as Governesses' by Hon. Lady Wilson, 1929, B.S.T., in *The Classics of
      Brontë Scholarship*, selected and introduced by Charles Lemmon, 1999, p. 221.
28   Taken from a letter from Charlotte Brontë to Ellen Nussey, 12 November 1840, MS
      n.1., [L & L, i,219], quoted by Juliet Barker in *The Brontës*, p.341.
29   Juliet Barker, *The Brontës*, p.342.
30   Elizabeth Franks died on 11th September 1837 just a year after Charlotte and
      Brontë's reluctant visit to her the previous June.
31   Margaret Oliphant's article 'The Condition of Women' in *Blackwood's Edinburgh
      Magazine 83*, February 1858, cited in the first Appendix on Charlotte M. Yonge's
      The Clever Woman of the Family, edited by Clare A. Simmons, p.551.
32   Harriet Martineau, 'Female Industry', *Edinburgh Review* 109 (April 1859). See
      appendix of Charlotte M. Yonge's *The Clever Woman of the Family*. p.553.
33   James R. Simmons, Jr., 'Class, Matriarchy and Power: Contextualizing the
      Governess in Agnes Grey', *New Approaches to the Literary Art of Anne Brontë*,
      edited by Julie Nash and Barbara A. Suess, (Ashgate Publishing Ltd., 2001), p.39.
34   Betty Jay, *Anne Brontë*, (Writers and their Work, 2000). See review of this by Mary
      Summers (*Brontë Transactions, Pt.2*, October 2000), Vol, 25, p.185.
35   *Anne Brontë's Agnes Grey: The Feminist; 'I must stand alone'*, by Bettina L. Knapp,
      New Approaches to the Literary Art of Anne Brontë, edited by Julie Nash and

Barbara A. Suess, (Ashgate Publishing Ltd., 2001), p.*64.*

36 Brontë made two diary notes about life at the Robinsons, the first after a few months: 'I dislike my situation and wish to change it for another'. (30 July 1841); the second reveals how disillusioned she was by what she had witnessed there: 'during my stay I have had some very unpleasant and undreamt of experience of human nature', (31 July 1845).

37 Mrs Elizabeth Gaskell, *Life of Charlotte Brontë*, edited by Alan Shelston, (Penguin Classics).

38 Taken from Anne Brontë's 'Preface to the Second Edition', written 22 July, 1848.

39 In *The Daily Telegraph*, Thursday, September 6, 2001, the Cardinal Cormac Murphy-O'Connor, Archbishop of Westminster, stated that there was indifference in Britain to Christian Values and to the Church.

40 Charlotte Brontë, *Biographical Notice of Ellis and Acton Bell (1850)*.

41 Winifred Gérin, *Anne Brontë* (Thomas Nelson & Sons, 1959), p.32.

42 For a recent article on this subject, see 'Contextualizing Anne Brontë's Bible' by Maria Frawley, *New Approaches to the Literary Art of Anne Brontë* edited by Julie Nash, and Barbara A. Suess, (Ashgate Publishing Ltd, 2001).

43 Thomas À Kempis, *Of The Imitation of Christ*, (Rivingtons' Edition, London).

44 Mary Waldron, *Jane Austen and the Fiction of her time*, p.84.

45 Hannah More, *Coelebs in search of a Wife, 1808*, (Thoemmes Press, 1995), introduced by Mary Waldron, Ch.1.

46 The Penguin Dictionary of Proverbs, 1984, p.177, 128:7.

47 *Coelebs in search of a Wife*, 1808, Chapter 31, p.156.

48 See Coventry Patmore's slightly later poem of that name, 1854-1856.

49 Quoted by E. Langland in *Anne Brontë: The Other One*, (Barnes and Noble, 1989), p.40.

50 Introduction, p.vii/viii to *Discipline* by Mary Brunton, introduced by Fay Wheldon, (Pandora Press, 1986).

51 Mary Brunton, *Discipline*, introduced by Fay Wheldon, (Pandora Press, 1986), pp.3-5.

52 *The Letters of Horace Walpole* (1905), p.337, letter 2956, Vol.XV. Quoted in Claire Tomalin, *The Life and Death of Mary Wollstonecraft:* p.10. Also in Janet Todd, *Mary Wollstonecraft: A Revolutionary Life,* (Columbia U.P., 1987).

53 Elizabeth Langland assures us that Hannah More was certainly familiar with Wollstonecraft's *Vindication* See *Anne Brontë, The Other One* by Elizabeth Langland, p.40.

54 Mary Wollstonecraft, *Mary, A Fiction*, edited by Gary Kelly, (O.U.P., Oxford), 1988, p.1.

55 See Jane Moore, *Mary Wollstonecraft*, Writers and their Work, (Northcote House, 1999) p.10.

56 See 'Thoughts on the Education of Daughters', in *The Works of Mary Wollstonecraft*, edited by Janet Todd and Marilyn Butler, (Pickering and Chatto, 1989), Vol. IV., p.25.

57 Jane Moore, *Mary Wollstonecraft*, Writers and their Work, (Northcote House, 1999), p.26.

58 Ibid, p.9.

59 See Elizabeth Langland, *Anne Brontë, The Other One*, p.39.

60 Penny Gay, 'Anne Brontë and the Forms of Romantic Comedy', *(Brontë Society Transactions, April 1998)*, Volume 23, Pt.1.

61 *Jane Austen the Complete Novels: Persuasion*, (BCA, Crown Publishers, 1999), p.1046.

62 Facts from Dr. Mary Waldron's paper on Jane Austen, Women's Study Group, University of London, Sept. 2002.

63 *Jane Austen, the Complete Novels*, (BCA, Crown Publishers, 1999), p.18.

64 See Elizabeth Langland, *Anne Brontë, The Other One,* p.97.

65 Written by Anne Brontë to precede her second edition of *TWH* on 22 July, 1848.

66 See *From Moral Man to Godly Man: "Mr. Locke" and Mr. B in Part 2 of Pamela,* by Dr. Lois A. Chaber, published in *Studies in Eighteenth Century Culture, Vol. 18, American Society for Eighteenth-Century Studies.* Locke advocated the teaching of children by example rather than by abstract rules, just as did Anne Brontë, who evidently followed his methods. See also 'Of Paternal Power' in *Social Contract, Essays by Locke, Hume and Rousseau,* intro. by Sir Ernest Baker, (O.U.P., London), chapter VI, page 47, 'all parents were . . . under an obligation to preserve, nourish and educate the children they had begotten, not as their own workmanship, but the workmanship of their own Maker, the Almighty, to whom they were to be accountable for them.'

67 Emily Mary Osborn, *Nameless and Friendless,* exh. 1857, oil on canvas, 88 x 103 cm, collection of Sir David Scott, kindly pointed out by Dr. Carol Banks of the University of Hertfordshire.

68 Lawrence Stone, *The Road to Divorce,* (O.U.P., England, 1530-1987).

69 *Believe not those who say,* Chitham, No. 58, pp.162/3.

70 See 1850, Biographical Notice of Ellis and Acton Bell by Charlotte Brontë.

71 See also Juliet Barker, *The Brontës,* (Phoenix, Orion, 1995), p.503: '*Anne broke new ground with her plain and unassuming heroine.*

72 *BST,* Vol.18, No.2, p.146.

73 For a discussion on this, see Dr. R. Barnard's 'Dickens and the Brontës', (*BST,* Oct 2000), Vol.25, Pt.2.

74 Juliet Barker, *The Brontës. A Life in Letters,* (Viking, The Penguin Group, 1997), pp.105/106.

75 Hon. Lady Wilson, 'The Brontës as Governesses', *Classics of Brontë Scholarship,* ed. by Charles Lemmon, 1999, p.221.

76 Rikky Rooksby, 'Swinburne and the Brontës' (BST,1997), Vol. 22, p.193. Swinburne found Anne Brontë's *Tenant 'ludicrously weak, palpably unreal, and apparently imitative'* of *Jane Eyre.* In Clement Shorter's presentation copy of an 1889 edition of *Jane Eyre,* he writes: *To A. C. Swinburne, who has done so much for the due recognition of Charlotte Brontë's genius.'* To this, I would add: '*And so little for Anne Brontë's!'*

77 See Winifred Gérin's *Introduction to The Tenant,* p.14.

78 Quoted by Maria H. Frawley of Woman's Mission Boston 1840, *BST,* 20.3.133 (1991), p.141.

79 Quoted by G. H. Lewes.

80 Anne Brontë, *Preface to the Second Edition of The Tenant of Wildfell Hall,* 27 July, 1848, p.30.

81 *Fragment* of 26 January 1844, Chitham, No 28, p.97.

82 *O God! if this indeed be all,* May 20 1845, Chitham, No. 39, p.111.

83 Anne Brontë, *Preface to the Second Edition,* p.30.

84 Juliet Barker, *The Brontës. A Life in Letters,* (Viking, The Penguin Group, 1997), pp.90/91. See also Joan Bellamy, *More Precious than Rubies,* Highgate Publications, 2002.

85 Betty Jay, *Anne Brontë,* Writers and their Work, (Northcote House 2000).

86 Joan Bellamy, 'A Note on Lady Morgan', Vol.25, Pt.2, October 2000, p.168.

87 Mary Waldron, *Jane Austen and the Fiction of her time,* p.119.

88 Lawrence Stone, *The Road to Divorce,* (O.U.P., England. 1530-1987).

89 *'The unorthodox George Eliot (Marian Evans) lived with the married George Henry Lewes journalist and German scholar'.* See A. N. Wilson, *The Victorians,* pub. 2002, pt.II, p.167.

Index